# Old Chinatown

# Also from Westphalia Press
## westphaliapress.org

# Old Chinatown

## Turn of the Century Photographs of San Francisco's Chinatown

## by Arnold Genthe & Will Irwin

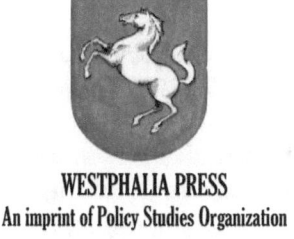

WESTPHALIA PRESS
An imprint of Policy Studies Organization

Westphalia Press
An imprint of Policy Studies Organization
1527 New Hampshire Ave., NW
Washington, D.C. 20036
info@ipsonet.org

ISBN-13: 978-1-63391-227-4
ISBN-10: 1633912272

Cover design by Taillefer Long at Illuminated Stories:
www.illuminatedstories.com

Daniel Gutierrez-Sandoval, Executive Director
PSO and Westphalia Press

Updated material and comments on this edition
can be found at the Westphalia Press website:
www.westphaliapress.org

# OLD CHINATOWN

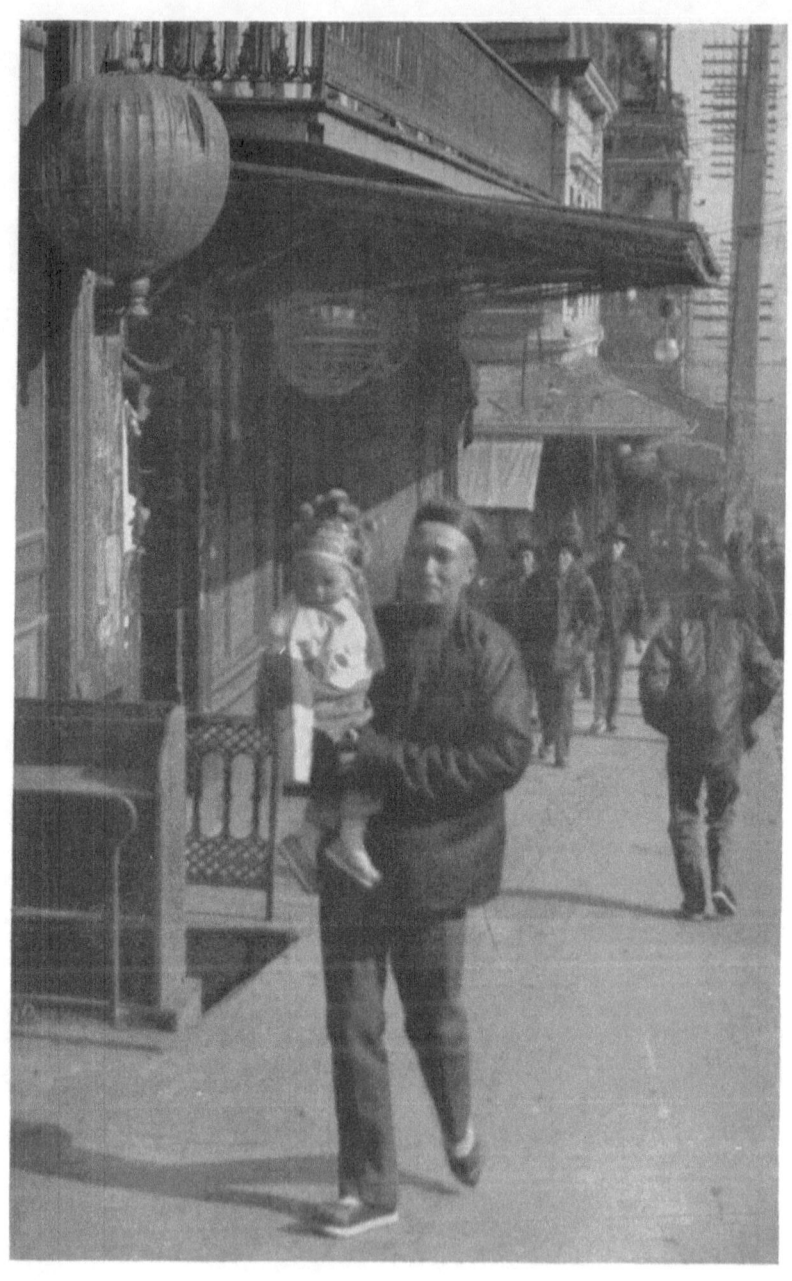

# OLD CHINATOWN

## A BOOK OF PICTURES BY
## ARNOLD GENTHE

### WITH TEXT BY
### WILL IRWIN

# OLD CHINATOWN PICTURES

# OLD CHINATOWN PICTURES

[ *viii* ]

# OLD CHINATOWN PICTURES

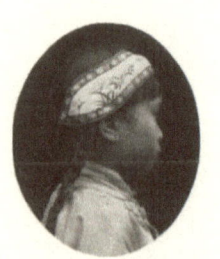

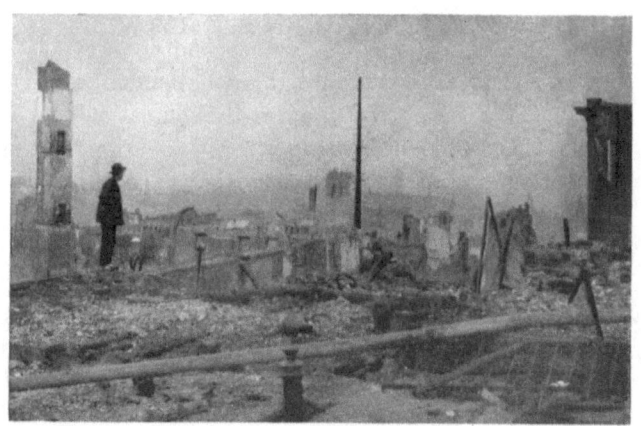

## FOREWORD

My Dear Dr. Genthe: — Long before I knew
who you were, I used to mark you in the shadows
and recesses of Chinatown, your little camera half-
hidden under your coat, your considering eye and
crafty hand of the artist alert to take your shy and
superstitious models unawares. Later, it was my
privilege to follow you sometimes — to watch you
playing your Germanic patience against their Chinese
patience, to marvel at you, in dark room and studio,
working with those mysterious processes by which
you — more than any other man alive — have
made art out of the play-time snap-shot. Now,
after the great disaster, all that you have saved of
your work of a decade is this same picture record
of old Chinatown at which you worked so lovingly.

In the summer of steel and steam drills and heroic
enthusiasm — the summer of rebuilding — you and
I passed through the new, clean Chinatown. It

was a clear, sea-scented night, I remember, and very late. We stopped beneath the ruins of Old St. Mary's. The new-rising city, like the old one in dim, suggestive contour — as an adult face is like its childish counterpart — stretched out at our feet. Where the vivid carouse and romance of Dupont and Kearny Streets had been, a black hollow, mysterious, awful, as though the Pit had taken Hell's Half Acre back to itself; beyond, a wall of steel skeletons and gaunt, windowless towers. The scattered lights, placed where never lights would be in finished and inhabited structures, gave a dreadful air of strangeness and desolation to this city vista. I stood as one who sees spirits. And you spoke:

"Rubber boots and kettles, overalls and blankets in the shop windows — and we have still to call it Chinatown!" You had been looking backward, I perceived, as I had been looking forward. So, with the skeleton of St. Mary's roof creaking above us in the night wind, we talked about that little city of our love, Chinatown. "No, it's gone," said I; "and beauty, or at least such beauty as they know, cannot live in Class A buildings." You, like a true partizan, fell to defending as soon as you found me agreeing with your criticisms. "They won't remain Class A for long," you said. "The Chinese will make them over somehow. They can no more live in inappropriate ugliness than we in dirt." Yet we both sighed for the Chinatown which we knew, and which is not any more except in the shadowing of your films.

You, the only man who ever had the patience to

[ *4* ]

# ARNOLD GENTHE

photograph the Chinese, you, who found art in the snap-shot — you had been making yourself unconsciously, all that time, the sole recorder of old Chinatown. I but write as a frame for your pictures; I am illustrating you. If, in these writings, I use the past tense, I do not mean to imply that our Californian Chinese have changed their natures or their manners. Much of what I describe here has survived, and much more will prevail. It is just that your lenses and plates record only the past; and, I, embroidering your work, have tried to keep in tone.

WILL IRWIN.

1908.

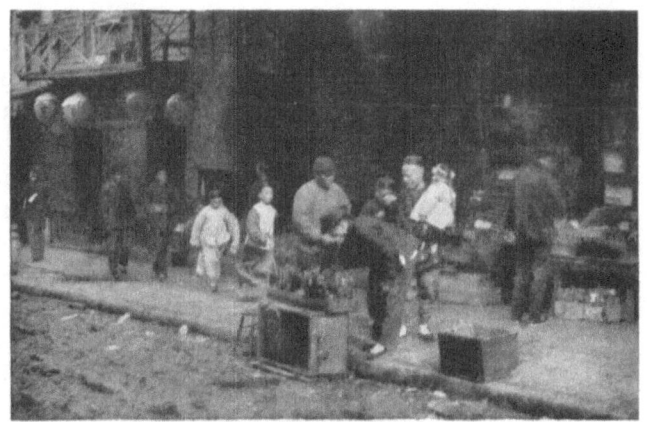

## CHAPTER ONE

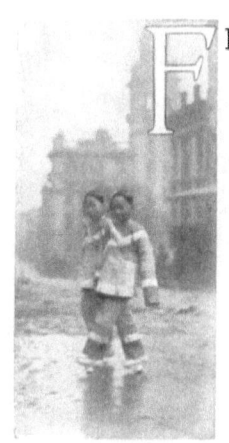

FROM the moment when you crossed the golden, dimpling bay, whose moods ran the gamut of beauty, from the moment when you sailed between those brown-and-green headlands which guarded the Gate to San Francisco, you heard always of Chinatown. It was the first thing which the guides offered to show. Whenever, in any channel of the Seven Seas, two world-wanderers met and talked about the City of Many Adventures, Chinatown ran like a thread through their reminiscences. Raised on a hillside, it glimpsed at you from every corner of that older, more picturesque San Francisco which fell to dust and cinders in the great disaster of 1906. From the cliffs which crowned the city, one could mark it off as a somber spot, shot with contrasting patches of green and gold, in the panorama below. Its inhabitants, overflowing into the American quarters, made bright and quaint the city streets. Its exemplars of art in common things, always before the unillumined American, worked to make San Francisco the city of artists that she was. For him who came but to look and to enjoy, this was the real heart of San Francisco, this bit of the mystic, suggestive East, so modified by the West that it was neither Oriental nor yet Occidental — but just Chinatown.

It is gone now — this Old Chinatown — but in a newer and stronger San Francisco rises a newer, cleaner, more healthful Chinatown. Better for the city — O yes — and better for the Chinese, who must come to modern ways of life and health, if they are to survive among us. But where is St. Louis Alley, that tangle of sheds, doorways, irregular arcades and flaming signs which fell into the composition of such a marvelous picture? Where is the dim reach of Ross Alley, that romantically mysterious cleft in the city's walls? Where is Fish Alley, that horror to the nose, that perfume to the eye? Where are those broken, dingy streets, in which the Chinese made art of rubbish?

I hope that some one will arise, before this generation is passed, to record that conquest of affection by which the California Chinese transformed themselves from our race-adversaries to our dear, subject people. Theirs will be all the glory of that tale, ours all the shame. In the dawn of the mining rush, the little, trading Cantonese began to appear in California. The American, the Celt, the

# ARNOLD GENTHE

Frenchman came for gold — gold washed out of the hills —uncounted millions. Gold brought the Chinaman also; but his ideas were modest. The prospect of two, four, five dollars a day was enough for him, who had made only ten cents a day at home. He asked simply to do menial work at a menial's wage. Beside our white pioneers, he took his part in the glorious episode of the Pacific conquest. He, with them, starved on the desert, died on the trails, faced Indian bullets and arrows. Wherever the report of gold called into being a new camp, he struggled in behind the whites, built his laundry, his cook-house or his gold rocker, girded up his pig-tail, and went to work. In his own spirit of quiet heroism, he shared all the hardships of our giant men — shared in everything they held except their dissipations and their reward of glory. For glory, he had to wait half a century.

That curious, black episode of early Western civilization, the Chinese persecution, followed hard upon their first arrival. Why this thing began, what quality in the Chinese nature irritated our pioneers beyond all justice and sense of decency, remains a little dim and uncomprehended to this generation. They were an honest people — honest beyond our strictest ideas. They attended to their own business and did not interfere with ours. Their immoralities, their peculiar and violent methods of adjusting social differences, affected only themselves. Not for thirty years was there reason for believing them a danger to American workingmen. But the fact remains. Our pioneers cast them forth disgraced, beat them, lynched them. Professional agitators made them a stock in trade. By the power of reiteration, this honest people came to figure in the public mind as a race of thieves, this cleanly people — inventors of the daily bath — as "dirty" and "diseased," this heroic people, possessed of a passive fortitude beside which our stoicism is cowardice, as poltroons. With a dignity all their own, they suffered and went about their business, though death lay at the end.

The day came when the Chinese themselves nearly justified the professional labor agitator. The romantic, unsettled period of the gold rush passed into history; the age of bonanza farming followed; the state buckled down to stable industry. But two and three and five dollars a day was still a lure to the Canton man. Their number increased with every Pacific steamer. Even yet they were no real menace to American labor — the state at any time might have swallowed up fifty thousand more without harming a single white workingman — but that menace lifted itself in the immediate future. Ripples from the black Dennis Kearney outrages, the shameful Montana massacres, reached Washington. Congress passed the Exclusion Law. When that happened, there vanished the last logical objection to the Californian Chinese.

A gradual change passed over the spirit of California. We were a long time learning that human souls, different but equal, souls softened by forty centuries of highly moral civilization, lay under those yellow skins, under those bizarre customs and beliefs. The Chinaman, being a gentleman, gives himself forth but charily. I think that we first

glimpsed the real man through our gradual understanding of his honesty. American merchants
learned that none need ever ask a note of a Chinaman in any commercial transaction. His word is
his bond. Precedent, as well as race characteristic,
makes it so.

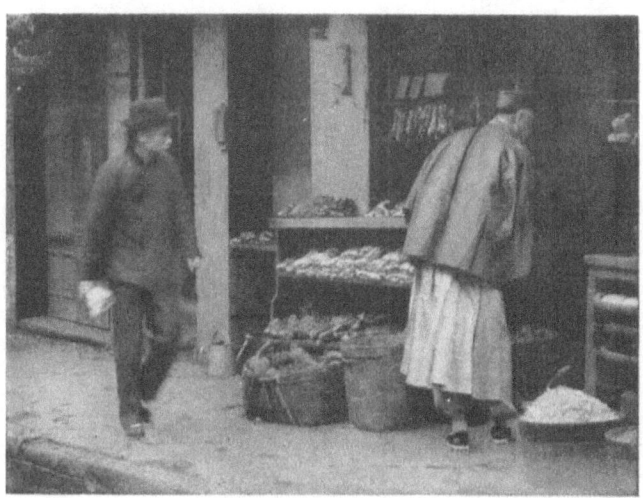

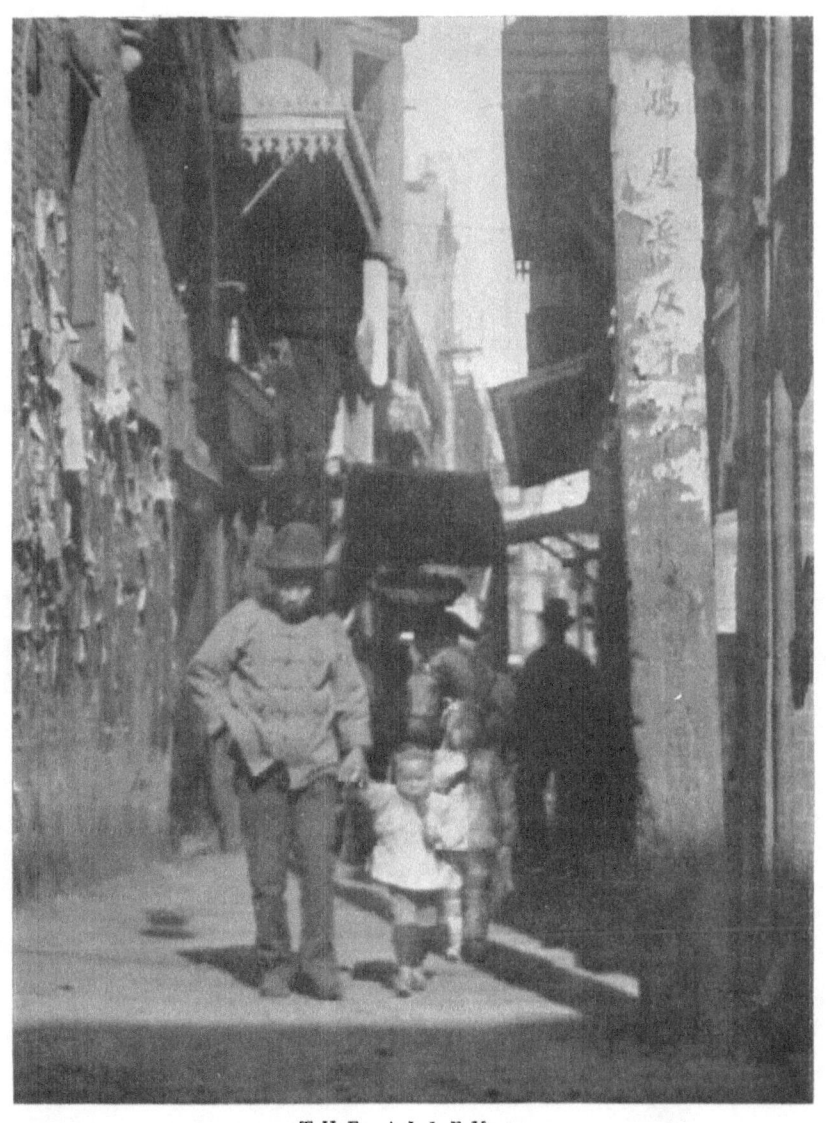

THE ALLEY

"THAT TANGLE OF SHEDS, IRREGULAR ARCADES AND FLAMING SIGNS"

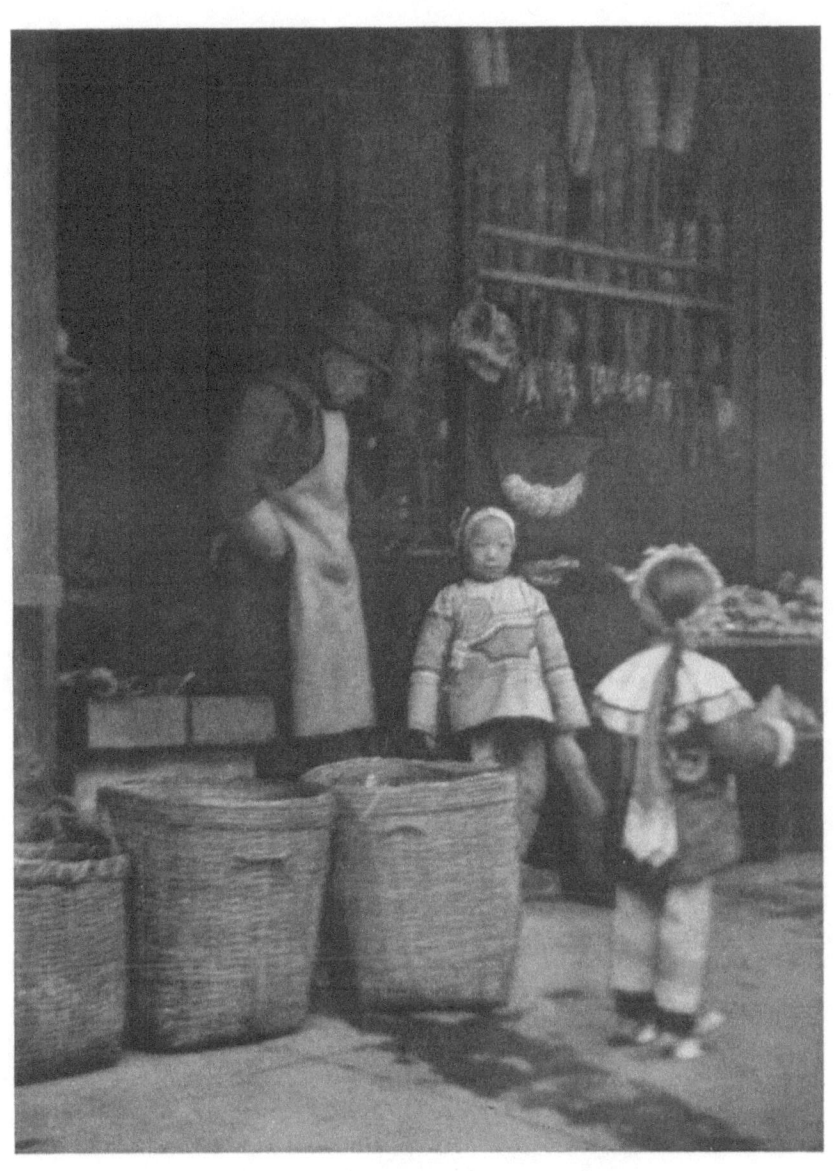

THE GROCERY STORE

15

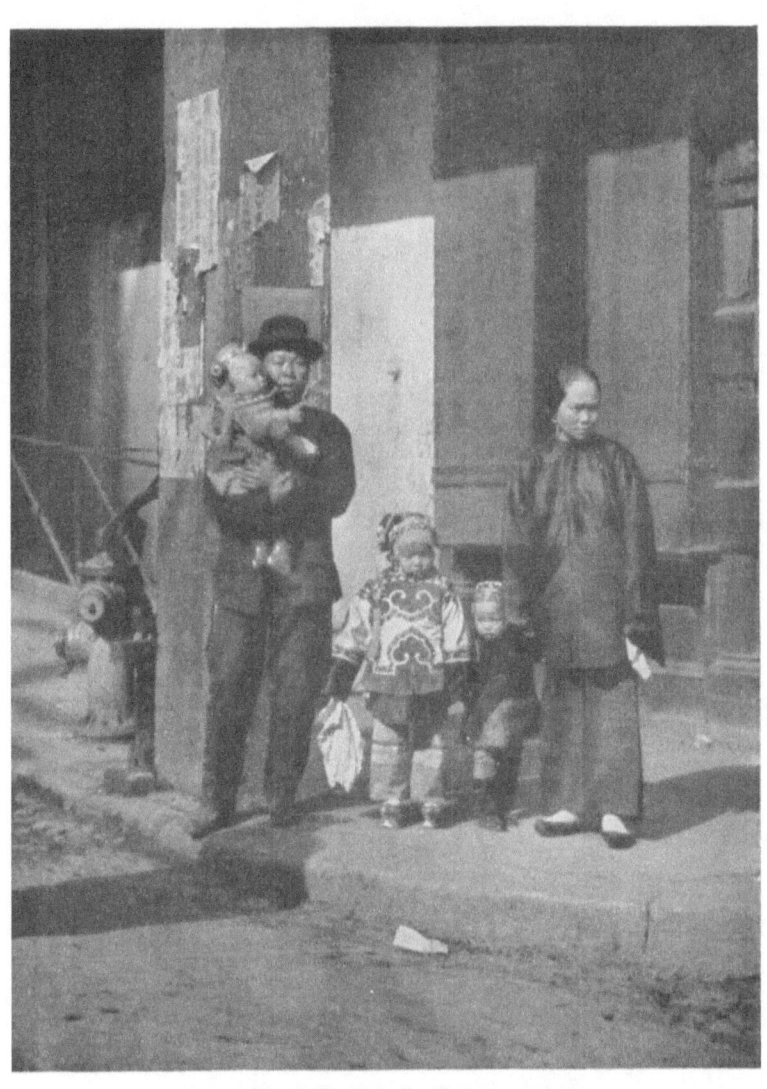

WAITING FOR THE CAR

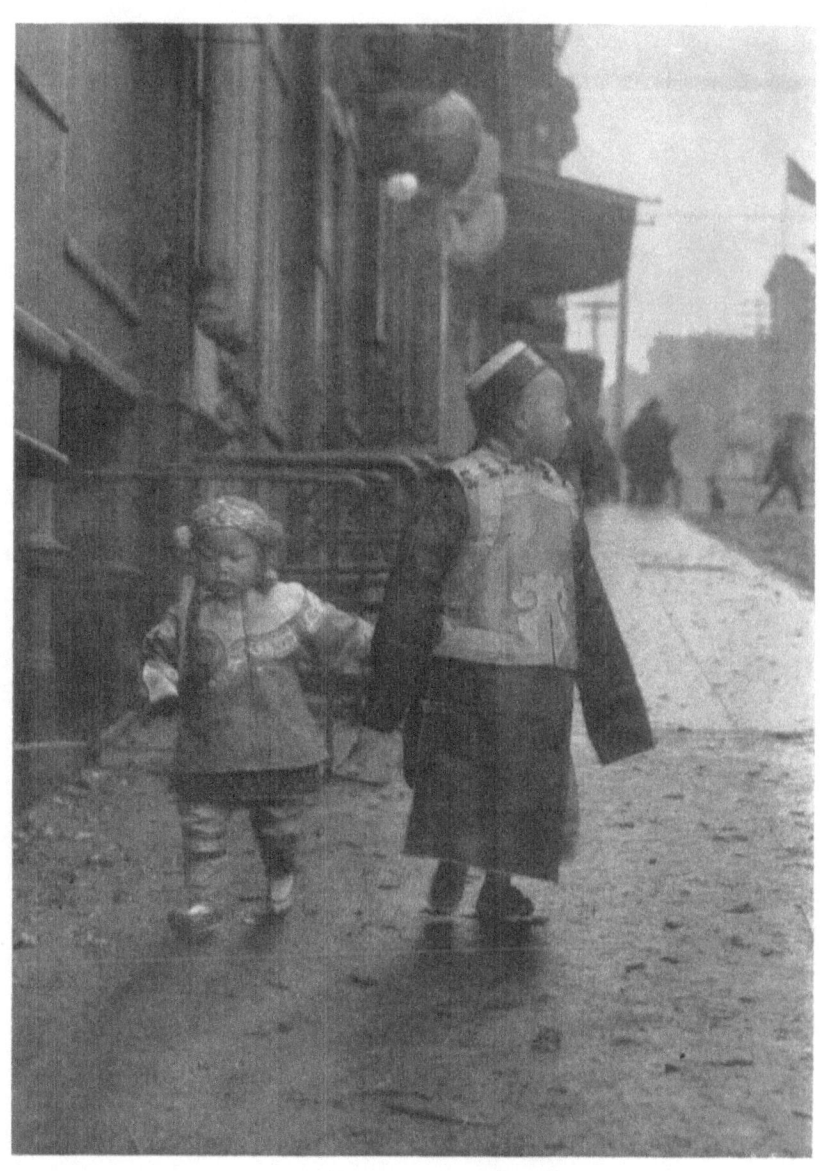

IN HOLIDAY DRESS

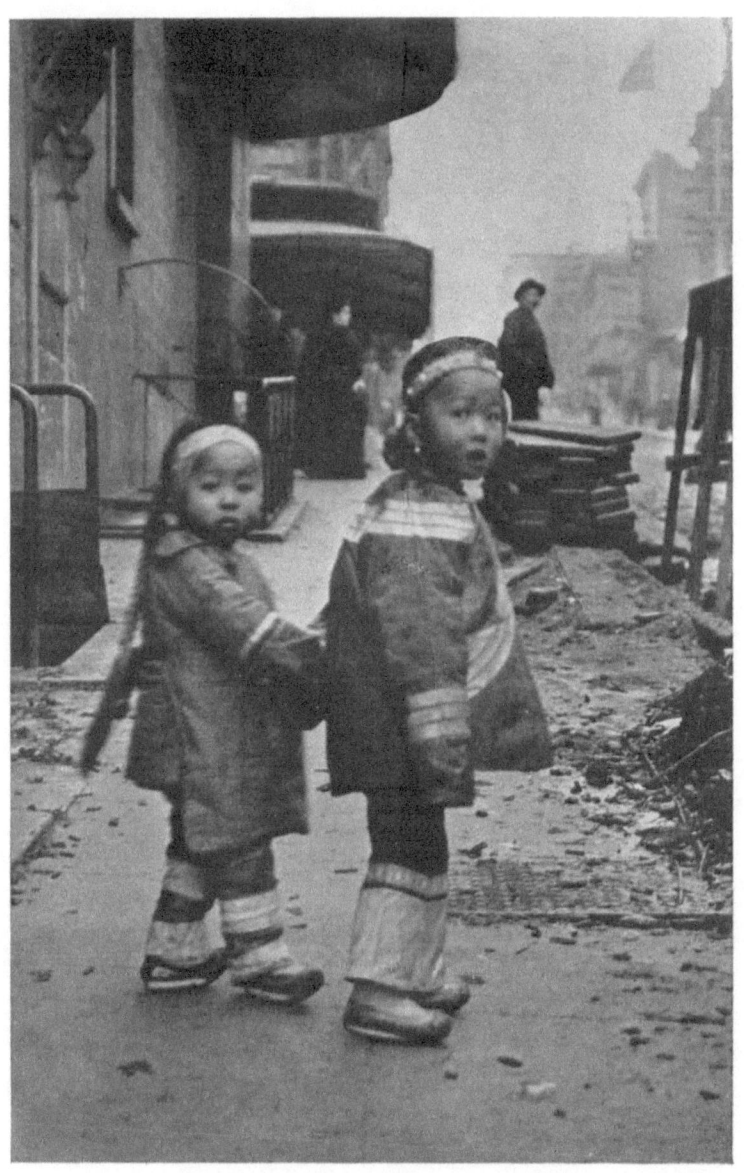

THEIR FIRST PHOTOGRAPH

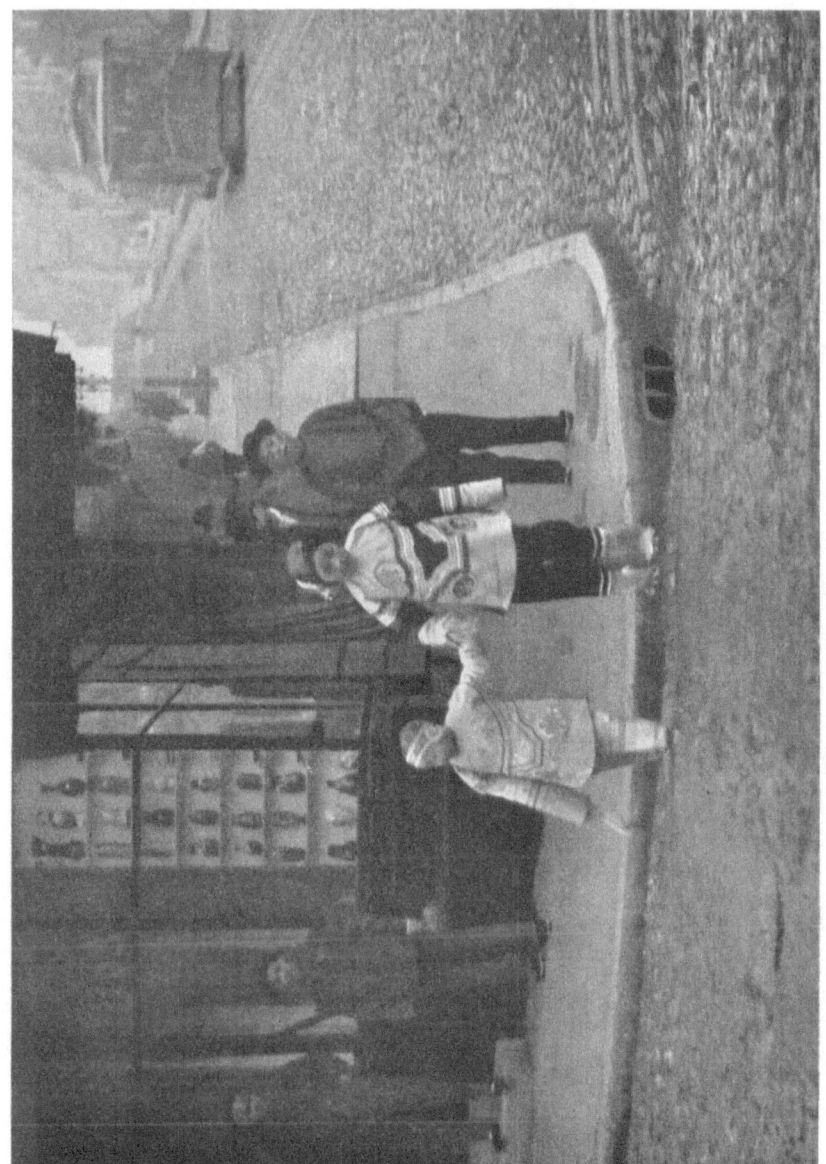

AT THE CORNER OF DUPONT AND
JACKSON STREETS

23

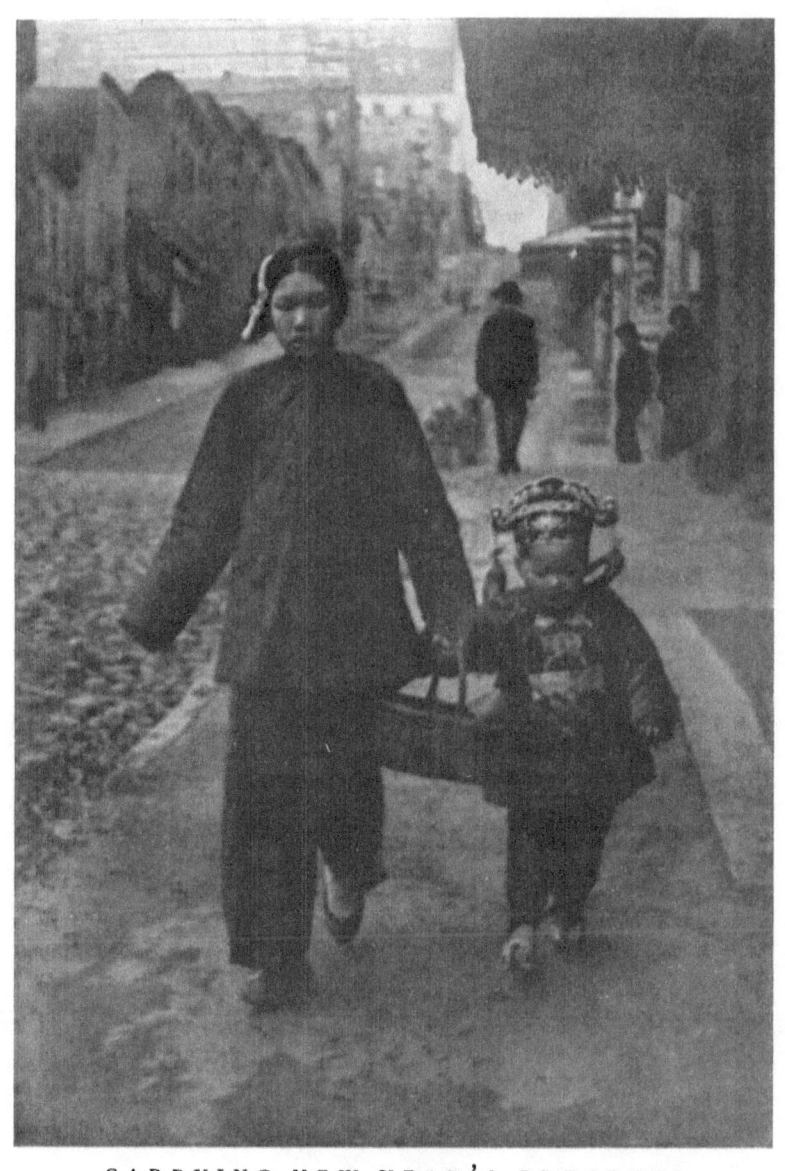

CARRYING NEW YEAR'S PRESENTS

## CHAPTER TWO

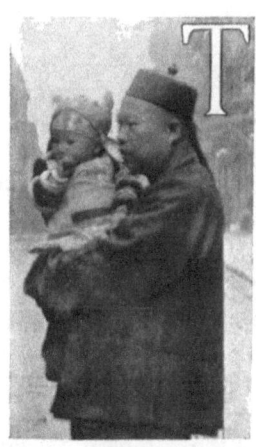

THE newer generation of Californians grew up with baby-loving, devoted Chinese servants about them. The Sons and Daughters of the Golden West did not, indeed, draw their first sustenance from yellow breasts, as the Southerner has drawn it from black ones. That mystic bond was lacking. But a Chinese man-servant had watched at the cradle above most of them, rejoiced with the parents that there was a baby in the house, laughed to see it laugh, hurried like a mother at its cry. A backyard picture in any of the old Californian mansions included always the Chinese cook, grinning from the doorway on the playing babies.

This Chinese cook was a volunteer nurse; for him, the nursery was the heart of the house. He was the consoler and fairy-teller of childhood. He passed on to the babies his own wonder tales of flowered princesses and golden dragons, he taught them to patter in sing-song Cantonese, he saved his frugal nickels to buy them quaint little gifts; and as the Southerner, despising the race, loves the individual negro through this very association of childhood, so the Californian came to love the Chinaman that he knew. In his ultimate belief, indeed, he outstripped the Southerner; for he came first to a tolerance of the race and then to an admiration.

The older people, and more especially the house-wives among them, reached understanding and admiration through a different channel. The China-man was an ideal servant. Now, when the insolent and altogether less admirable Japanese are taking their places beside the cook stoves, your San Francisco housewife will never cease lamenting for the old order. His respect for a contract, written or spoken, made him observe every article of the servant's code. Unobtrusive, comprehending in all its subleties the feminine mind, part of the house-hold and still aloof from it, the Chinese servant did the work of two American maids and stirred up no friction in the process. Supreme virtue of all to his mistress, he delighted in "company," in all the pomps and parades of a household. Nothing pleased him more than to take the responsibility of a dinner or a reception upon himself, to plan confections for it, to have a hand in the decorations. The other side of his life, which might be frescoed with fan-tan and highbinder troubles, he kept for Chinatown and his night off. Perhaps on that night he dropped his month's wages in the gambling houses of Ross Alley, perhaps he smoked a few pipes of opium, perhaps he knew more than the police would ever learn of the highbinder shooting proclaimed all across the first page of that newspaper which he calmly handed you at breakfast. He never troubled you with these things. To you, he was first the perfect servant, and, if his term lasted long enough, the shy, and gentle familiar, versed in the arts of friendship. Who more gracious than your Chinese cook or laundryman calling on Chinese New Years, his hands full of lilies for the women of the family, his pockets of nuts for the children? So, out of family life, both child and parent learned to appreciate and love the race. The Chinese had conquered our foolish hatred by patient service.

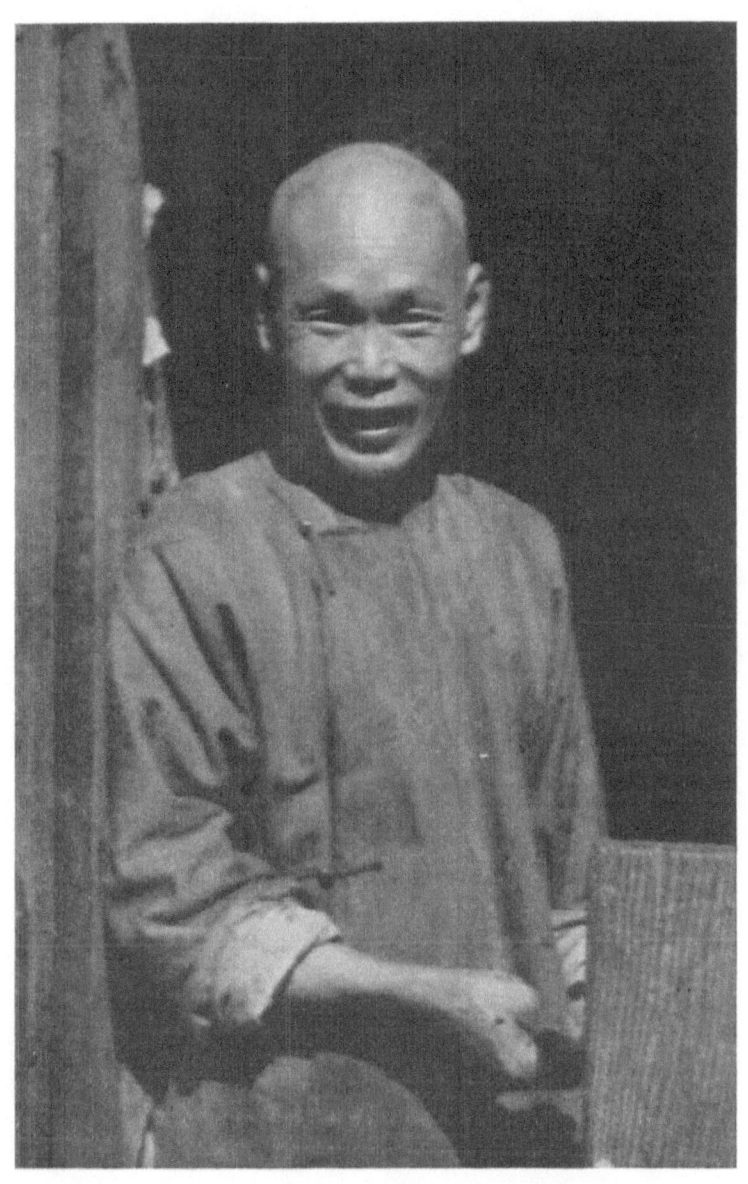

"THE CHINESE COOK, GRINNING
FROM THE DOORWAY"
31

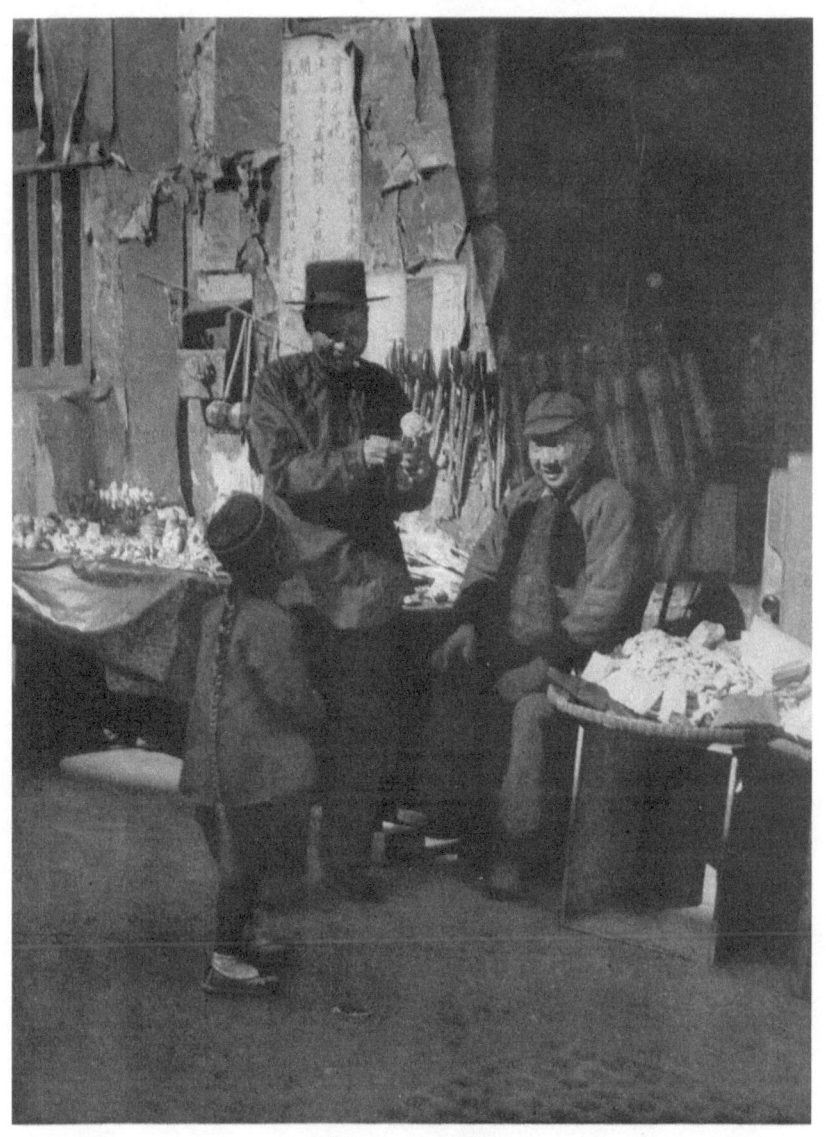

THE NEW TOY

33

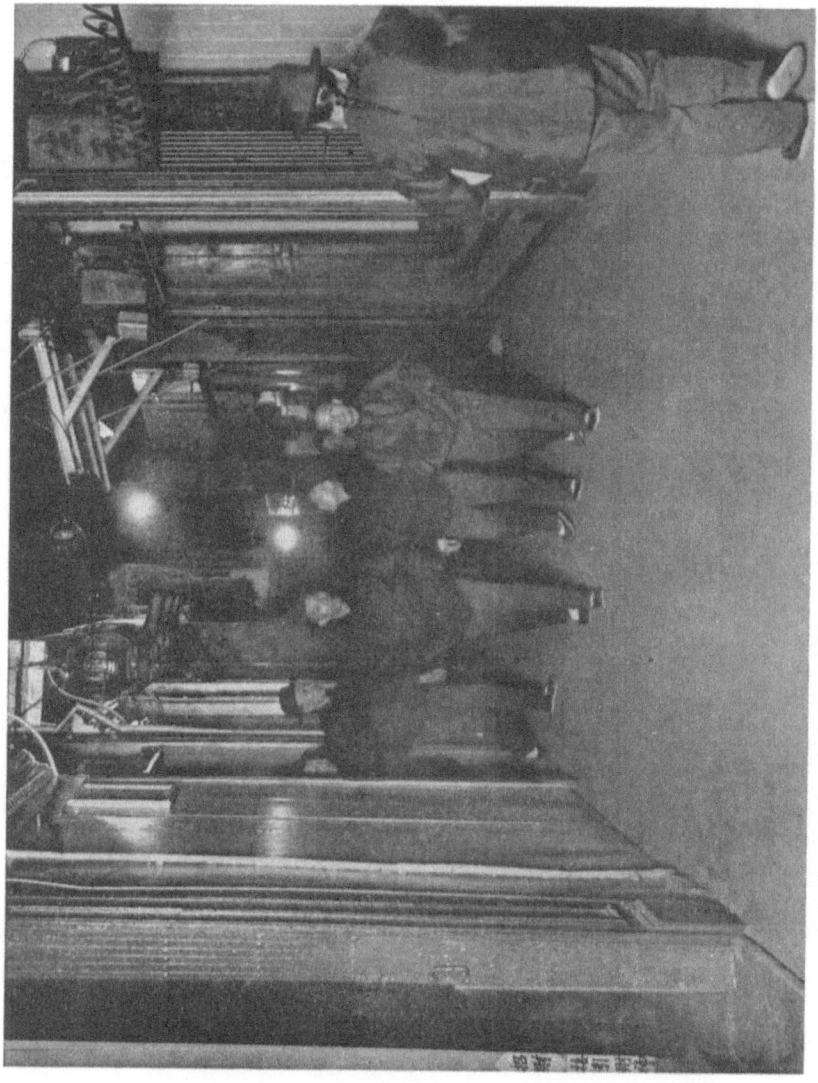

THE STREET OF THE GAMBLERS [BY NIGHT]

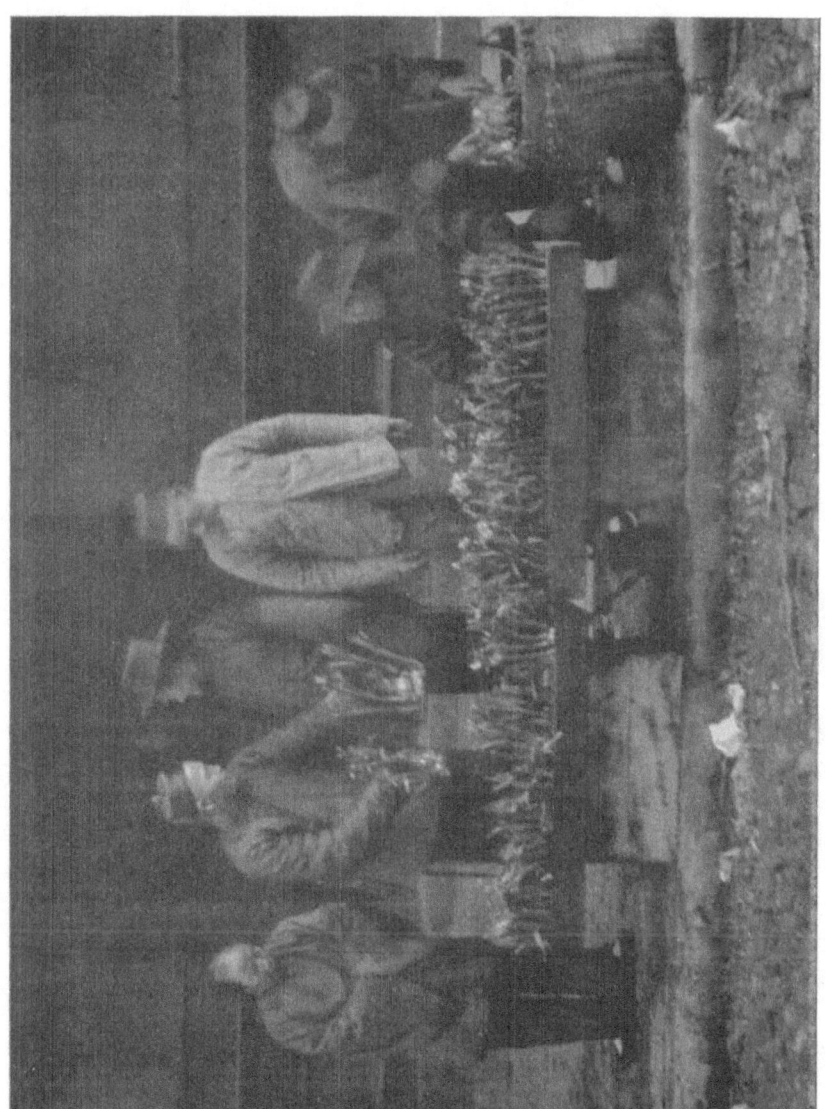

THE LILY VENDOR

37

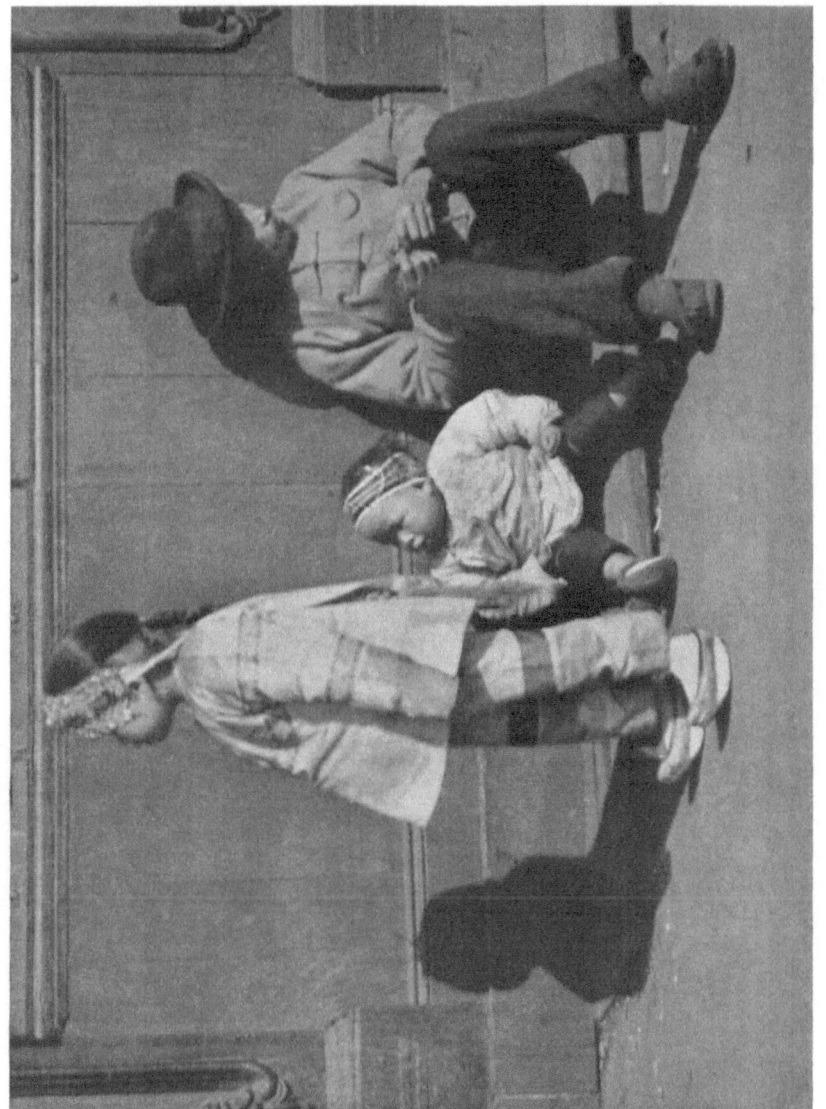

AN AFTERNOON SIESTA

39

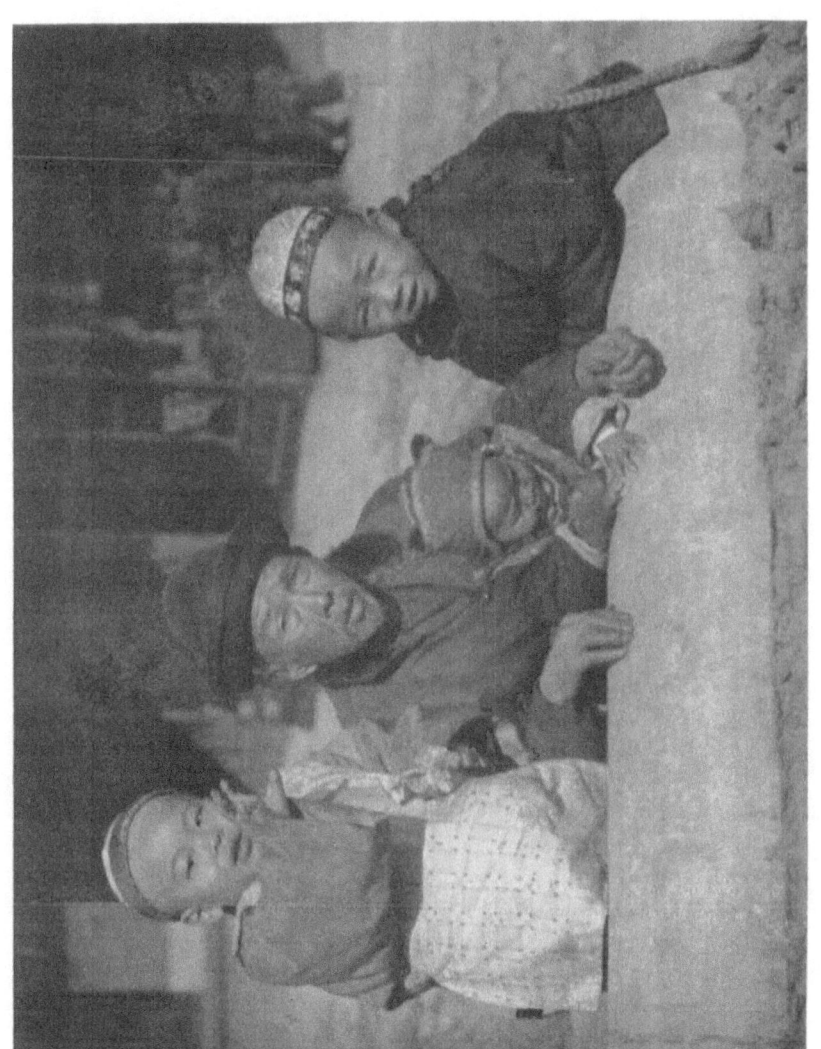

# CHAPTER THREE

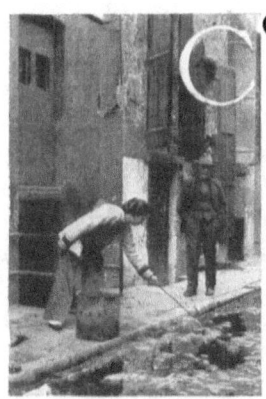

OMMENCING like all Spanish towns, San Francisco clustered first about a plaza — Portsmouth Square the pioneers renamed it. On its fringes, in the days when the streets ran gold and the Vigilantes were the whole law, appeared the first modern buildings. Then, with the unaccountable, restless drift of American cities, shops and wholesale houses passed on down into the hollows and "made lands" reclaimed from the Bay marshes. The Chinese, following in, took possession of those old buildings about Portsmouth Square. An unwritten city ordinance, strictly observed by successive Boards of Supervisors, held them to an area of about eight city blocks. Old St. Mary's Church, the first Roman Catholic Cathedral, marked the southern edge of that area; and to the last day of the old city any report that the Chinese were moving south of St. Mary's drove the newspapers and the city fathers to arms. The Chinese conquest of affection never proceeded so far that the Americans wanted them for neighbors.

These eight blocks, supporting a population which varied between ten thousand and thirty thousand according to the season of the year, lay close to the very center of San Francisco, between the business district and the old palaces of Nob Hill. Wealthy citizens, walking down to their offices from the citadel of the town, used to envy the Chinese their site; the city authorities were forever starting a movement to get "dirty Chinatown" out into the suburbs, that the whites might take the Quarter back. But the Chinese owned much of the property, and paid a high rental for the rest. With their conservatism and their persistence, they stuck. They stuck even after the fire, when San Francisco, starting a dozen projects in the heroic rebound of its spirit, tried to seize the occasion to move Chinatown.

This district of old-fashioned business blocks, laid out on fine lines by the French architects who wrought before the newly-rich miners began to buy atrocities, the Chinese transformed into a semblance of a Chinese city. They added sheds, lean-tos, out-door booths, a thousand devices to extend space; they built in the eternal painted balconies of which the Chinaman is as fond as a Spaniard. Close livers by custom, they lodged twenty coolies in one abandoned law office; they even burrowed three stories underground that they might make space for winter-idle laborers, overflow of the northern canning factories. Clinging always to their native customs and dress and manners, they furnished their little stores and factories, their lodging houses, their restaurants, with the Chinese utensils of common life which were never without their touch of beauty.

So the Quarter grew into a thing like Canton and still strangely and beautifully unlike. Dirty — the Chinaman, clean about his person, inventor of the daily bath, is still terribly careless about his surroundings. Unsanitary to the last degree — Chinatown was the care and vexation of Boards of Health. But always beautiful — falling everywhere into pictures.

This beauty appealed equally to the plain citizen, who can appreciate only the picturesque, and to the artist, with his eye for composition, subtle coloring, shadowy suggestion. From every doorway flashed out a group, an arrangement, which suggested the Flemish masters. Consider that panel of a shop front in Fish Alley which is to me the height of Dr. Genthe's collection. Such pictures glimpsed about every corner. You lifted your eyes. Perfectly arranged in coloring and line, you saw a balcony, a woman in softly gaudy robes, a window whose blackness suggested mystery. You turned to right or left; behold a pipe-bowl mender or a cobbler working with his strange Oriental tools, and behind him a vista of sheds and doorways in dim half tone, spotted with the gold and red of Chinese sign-boards. Beautiful and always mysterious — a mystery enhanced by that green-gray mist which hangs always above the Golden Gate and which softens every object exposed to the caressing winds and gentle rains of the North Pacific.

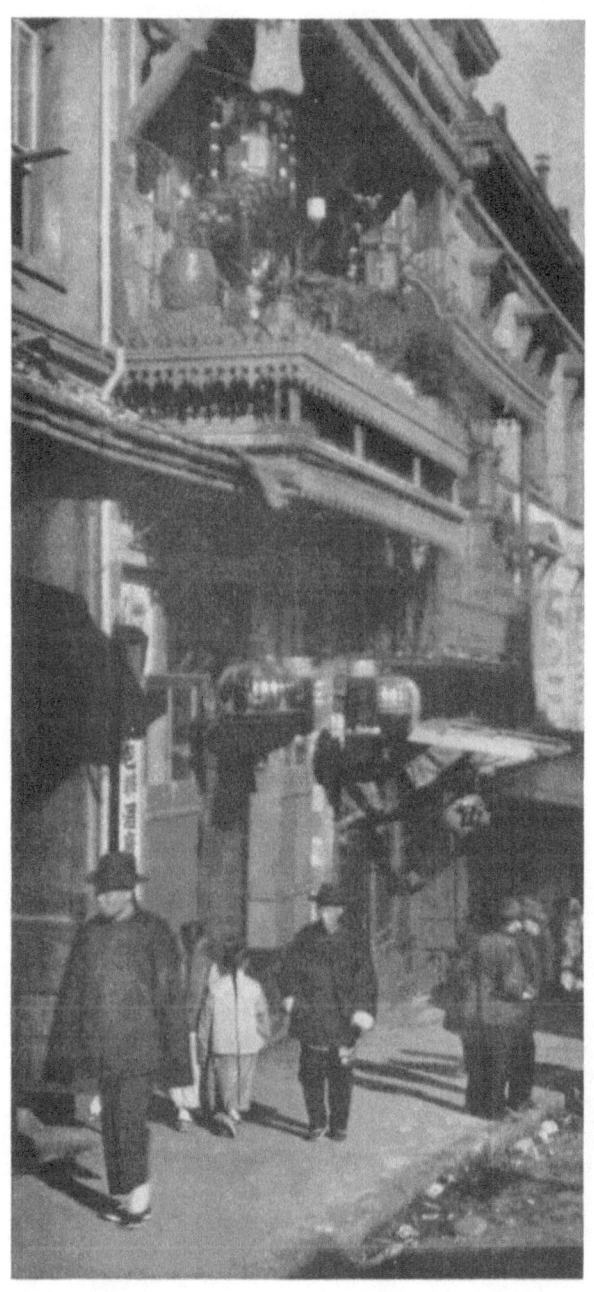

THE STREET OF PAINTED
BALCONIES

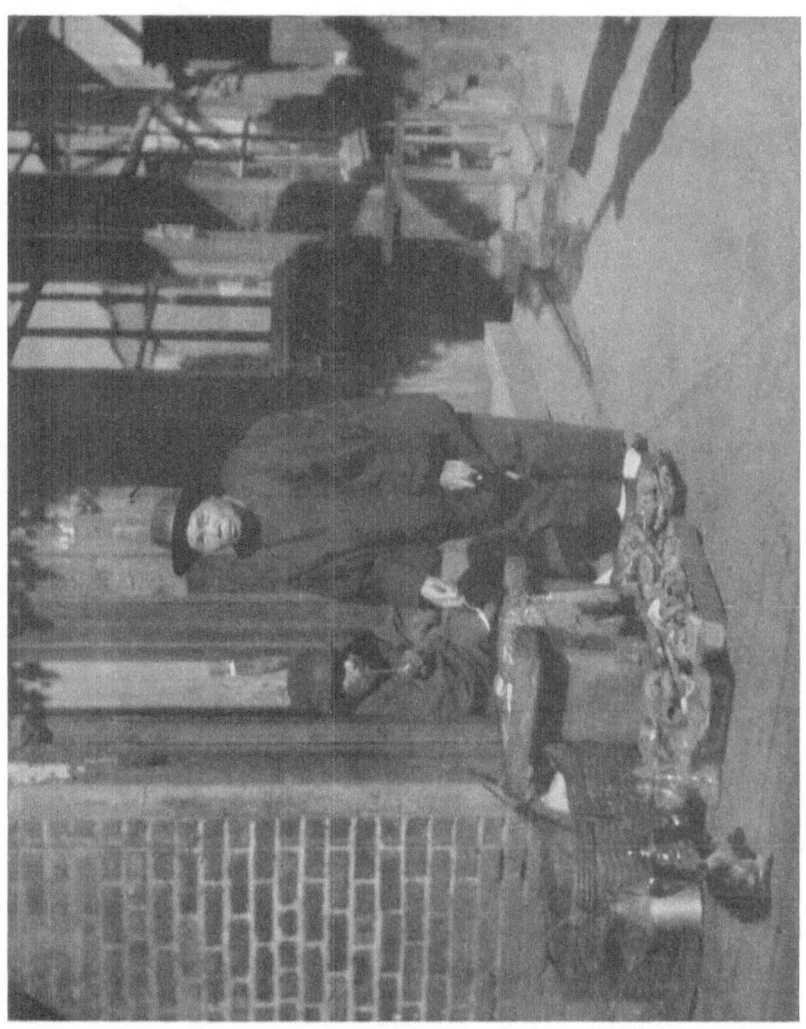

THE TINKERS

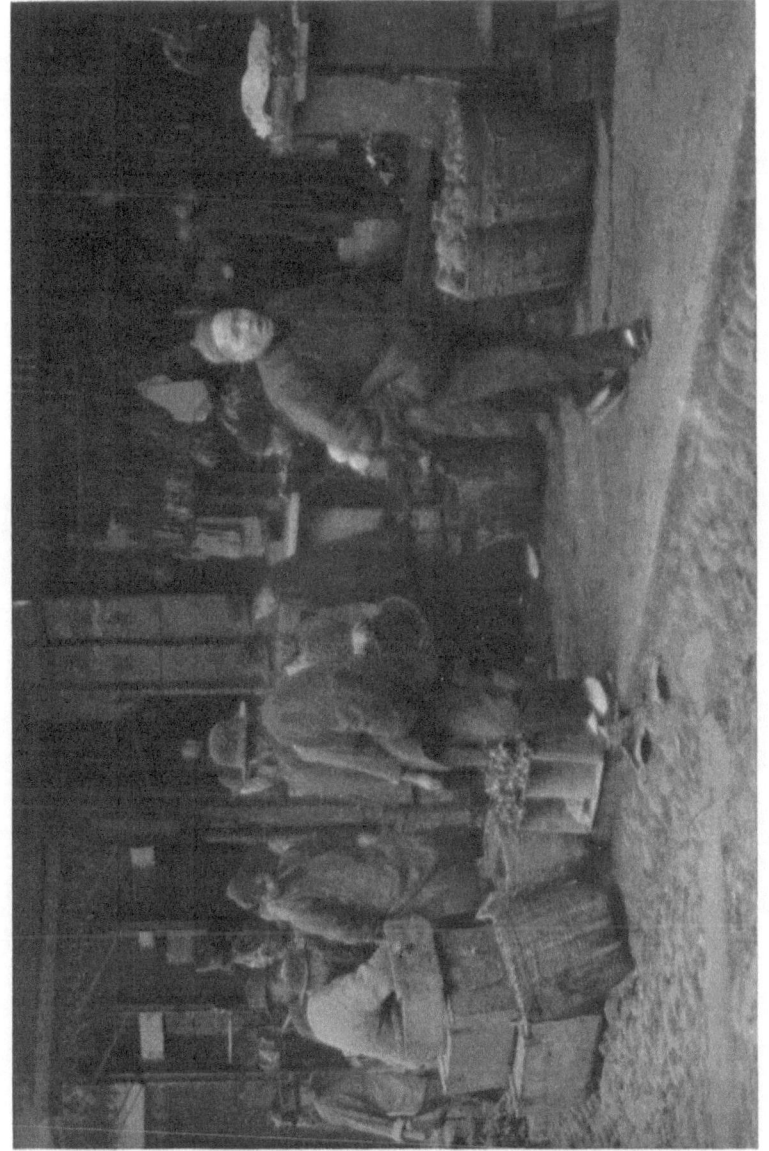

THE MORNING MARKET

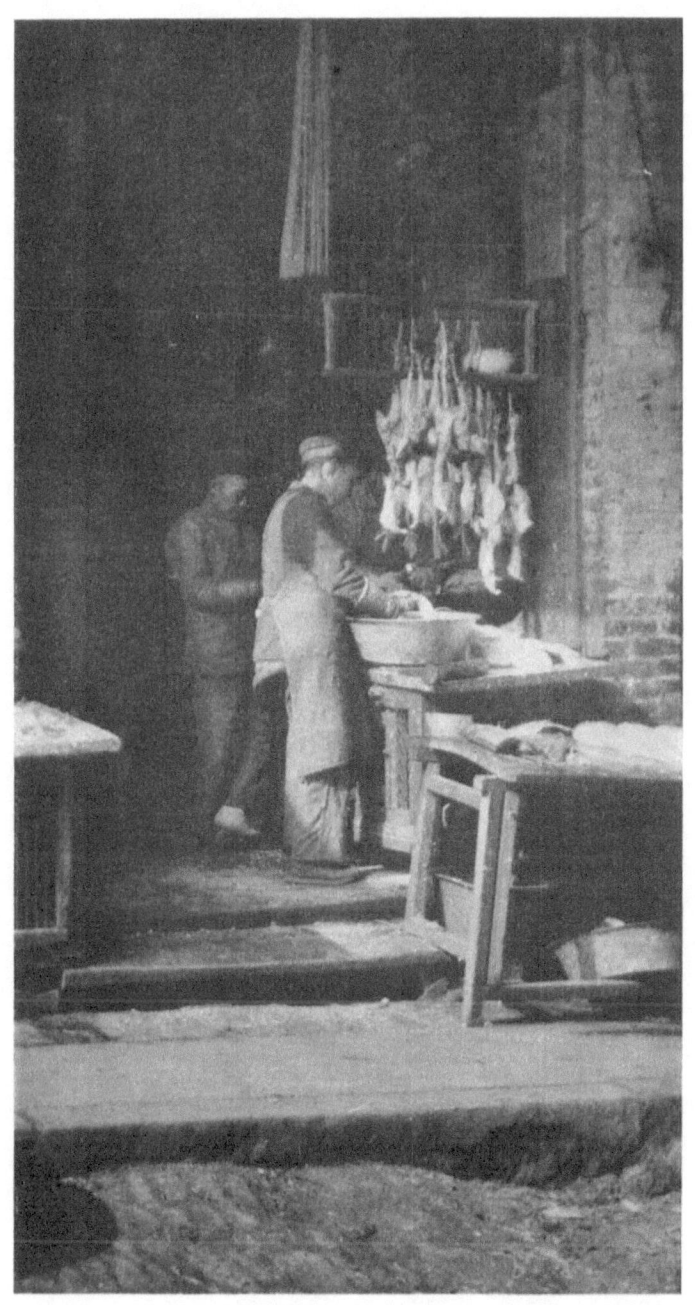

FISH ALLEY

"THAT HORROR TO THE NOSE, THAT PERFUME TO THE EYE"

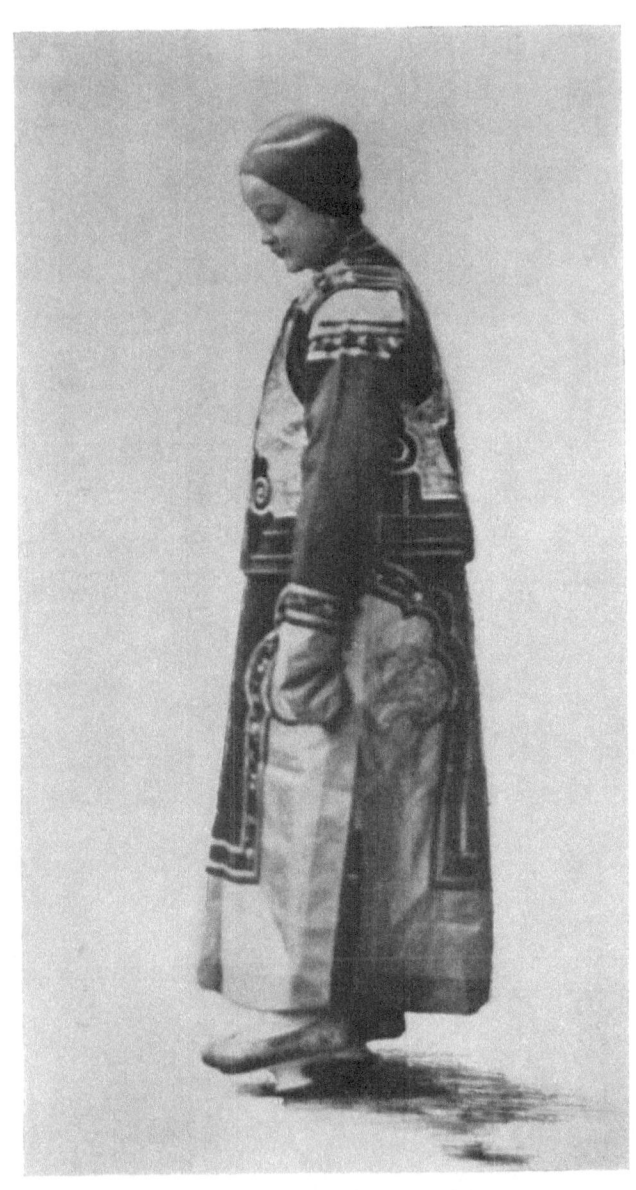

DRESSED FOR A FORMAL VISIT

55

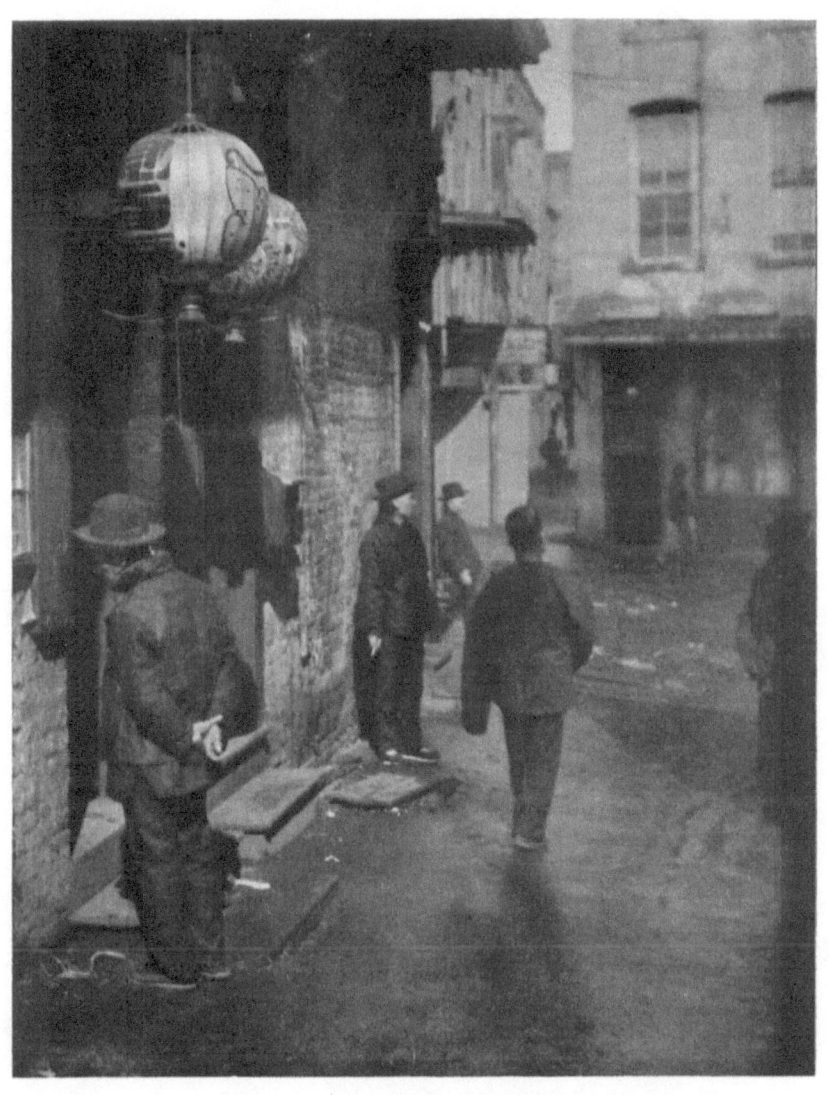

DOORWAYS IN DIM SHADOWS

57

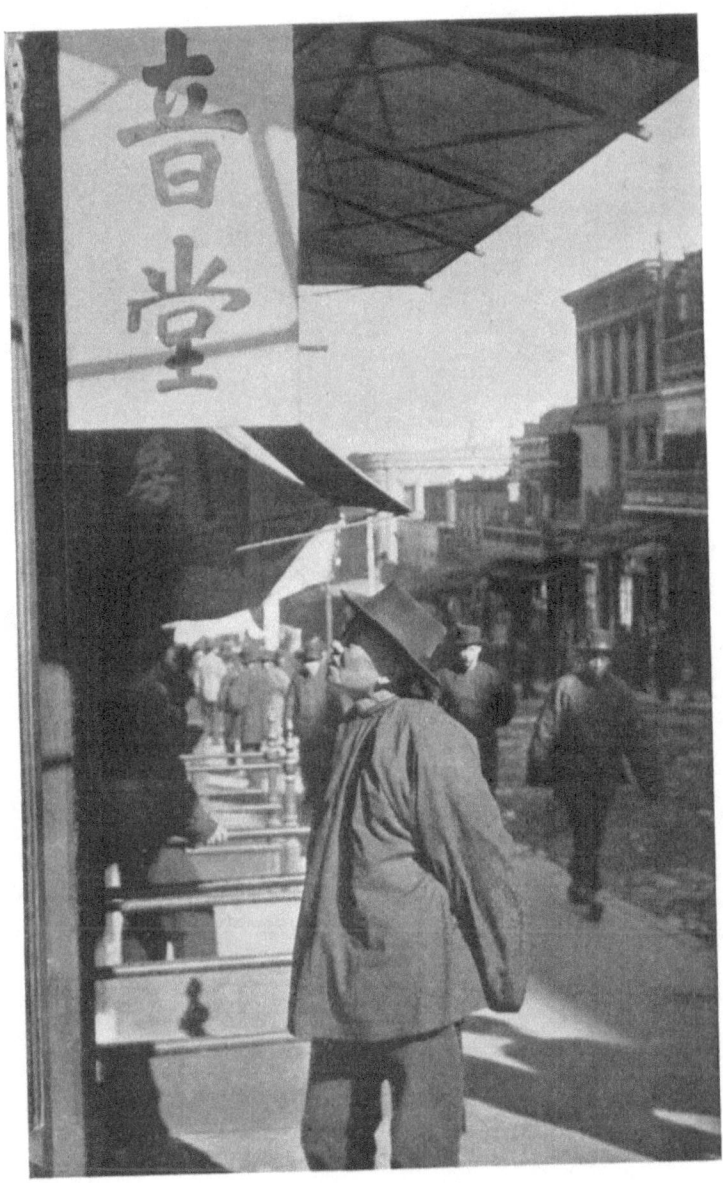

PASSERS-BY

59

## CHAPTER FOUR

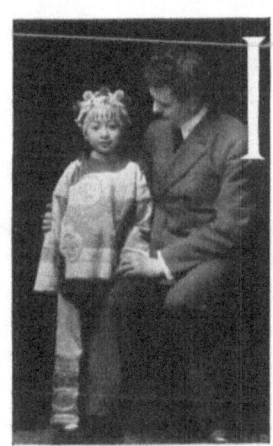

IN the greatest of his short stories, Frank Norris said that there were three circles in Chinatown. The first was the life of the streets, which never grew stale to the real Californian. The second was that prepared show which the tourist saw and which supported those singular persons, the Chinatown guides. The third was a circle away down below, into which no white man, at least none who dared tell about it, ever penetrated — the circle which revolved about their trafficking in justice, as they conceived of justice, about their trade in contra-band goods, such as opium and slave girls.

Rather, I think, were there four circles, for in between the circle of Show Places and that of Hidden Things came the family life and industrial activity of the Quarter.

This Chinatown was a Tenderloin for the whole Chinese population of the Pacific Coast, the pleas-

ure palace where fish cutters from the northern
salmon canneries, farmers from the Sacramento
deltas, fruit pickers from the hot San Joaquin, gold
washers from the mountains, came to enjoy themselves and to squander their earnings between
seasons.  Although a part of its reputed vicious-
ness was the exaggeration of race hatred, no man
could deny that it was tough.  Also, it had gathered
about it the lowest of those white tramps and sol-
diers of ill fortune who haunted that terminus of
Caucasian civilization, San Francisco.  The habita-
tion of a darker race has an attraction for the de-
based; witness the environs of negro streets in the
South.  Because "sin is news and news is sin," this
side of Chinatown was always before the public.

Nevertheless, a real life of homes and quiet industry went on there also.  The Chinese overall,
cigar and shoe factories were important enough to
draw the hatred of labor unions for a generation.
Much of the American tea and silk trade was con-
trolled from those streets.  The Six Companies,
virtually the Chinese Chamber of Commerce —
though bound by an alliance closer than any commercial organization which we know — had but to
assert itself, and the whole Pacific Coast paid atten-
tion.  The merchants, as they grew rich, sent to
China for their old wives, married new ones by
proxy, slipped brides past the inspectors, bought
them from the slave dealers.

To a degree which we cannot comprehend, the
place of the respectable Chinese woman is in
the home.  So the foreign American seldom saw
the true lady of the Chinese Quarter.  She lived

close to her home, she bound her hair with sober fillets, she dressed quietly, and she went abroad only on great business or on the occasion of great festivals.

But children, — high and low, rich and poor, they had the run of the streets. And they were the pride, joy, beauty and chief delight of the Quarter. Hope of heaven and everlasting worship to their fathers, nothing was too bright and beautiful for them. So mothers and nurses decked them out in the brightest tunics, the most cleverly conceived caps, all tinkling with golden devil-chasers, the whitest little socks and shoes, the most gorgeous ear-tassels, fit, otherwise, only for the altars of the joss. Tiny, yellow flowers of the world — how the American women, native and tourist, used to crane their necks and smile and coo at them as they passed! With what pride the father — never the mother — used to carry the boy baby down the streets in all his finery! How the Chinese, child lovers from the bottoms of their hearts, used to pay them court on the corners! Usually, they were contented and rather stolid babies; only once in a blue moon did one of them cry. And when it happened that a baby cried on the streets, the Chinese, bargaining at the open shop fronts, used to look after him and grin and exchange comments in Cantonese sing-song as though it was the greatest joke in the world.

School, whether in the Oriental schoolhouse which the city maintained or in the private Chinese seminaries of the rich and conservative, was out by four o'clock. That was the brightest hour of all the day in those streets. Dupont and Washington and

Stockton blossomed with racing, tumbling babies, all bright in silks. The barber, the grocer, the butcher, the lantern maker, dropped tools and occupation and came to the doorways to watch them play. The elder sisters walked arm on waist like school-girls the world over, swaying with that gentle motion which marks the Chinese lady from her common sister. The big boys, much more subdued than our own twelve year olds, got out those feathered shuttlecocks with which the Chinese youth imitates football, and frisked along Dupont Street or over into Portsmouth Square. A curious game that was, without team work or rules — nothing to it but dexterity of foot. Something essentially Oriental in its grotesque grace appeared in the attitudes of these boys as they kicked the ball, first forward like the punt of a Rugby player, and then backward over their shoulders like a French movement in *la savate*. Sometimes the more radical mothers joined their babies after school, walked down to the Square — a fearful journey for them — and made a little picnic about the football players. That children's hour of the Quarter showed Chinatown at its sweetest and most gracious.

Once only, in my recollection, came a day when all the women, high and low, had free run of the streets. This was the Good Lady Festival, celebrated every seven years in honor of that illustrious Chinese woman, princess and martyr, who was raised for her virtues to godhood. Her symbol is the little shoe, the tapering shoe of the lily feet, which she threw into the river before she died. And on the day of her festival, woman was raised to the level of man. She was free to walk the streets, to sacrifice, to bow publicly before the outdoor altars where priests tapped their little gongs and sang incessantly to the joss. The "Prayer store" on Dupont Street, where one might buy anything and everything sacred to Chinese religion, banked its counter and filled its windows with shoes of all sizes and colors.

On that day, also, did the respectable woman wear those multi-colored robes, those trousers of pale, neutral shades, those jade and gold ornaments for the hair, publicly appropriate at other times only to the women of no caste. From the brass and cedar treasure chests kept carefully under the beds in their tiny flats, they took these festival clothes, saved, perhaps, since the wedding; and Chinatown became one blaze of color. Here, as everywhere else, fashions changed; one marked that phenomenon usually by the variations in the children's caps and the colors and decorations of the tunics worn by the women. The black, straight hair, glossy with ointments, was usually bound by a great clasp of hammered gold which amounted almost to a cap.

Down the street, that night, walked a procession of priests in white robes. They carried a great banner inscribed with decorative Chinese characters; to right and left of them walked stavemen bearing weapons of the old Empire. Behind followed the women, for all the world like a swaying bed of great, gaudy flowers. Along the sidewalks burned unnumbered sacrificial candles and lights, surrounding the roast pig and rice bowls of a

Chinese sacrifice. When the procession was over, the women, emancipate for the night, went to feast — those of no caste to the restaurants, the ladies to their somber homes.

Next morning, when the careful priests of Confucius had picked up the papers on the streets and burned them, that the sacred characters might not be sullied by base uses, the women were back in their nests again, soberly dressed, keeping close that they might not dishonor their lords through the glance of forbidden eyes; and only the harlot and the very young maiden walked freely and frequently abroad until their next holiday.

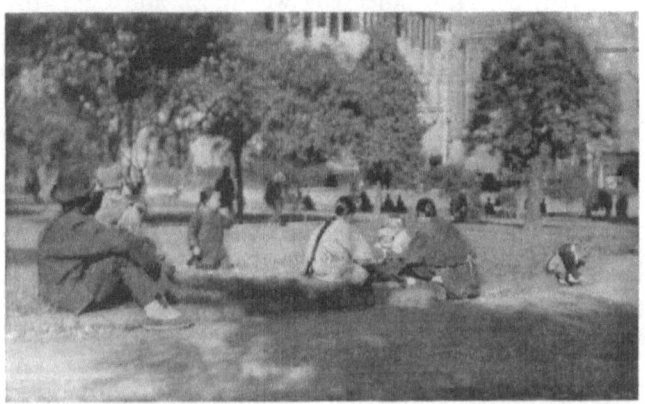

A CORNER CROWD

69

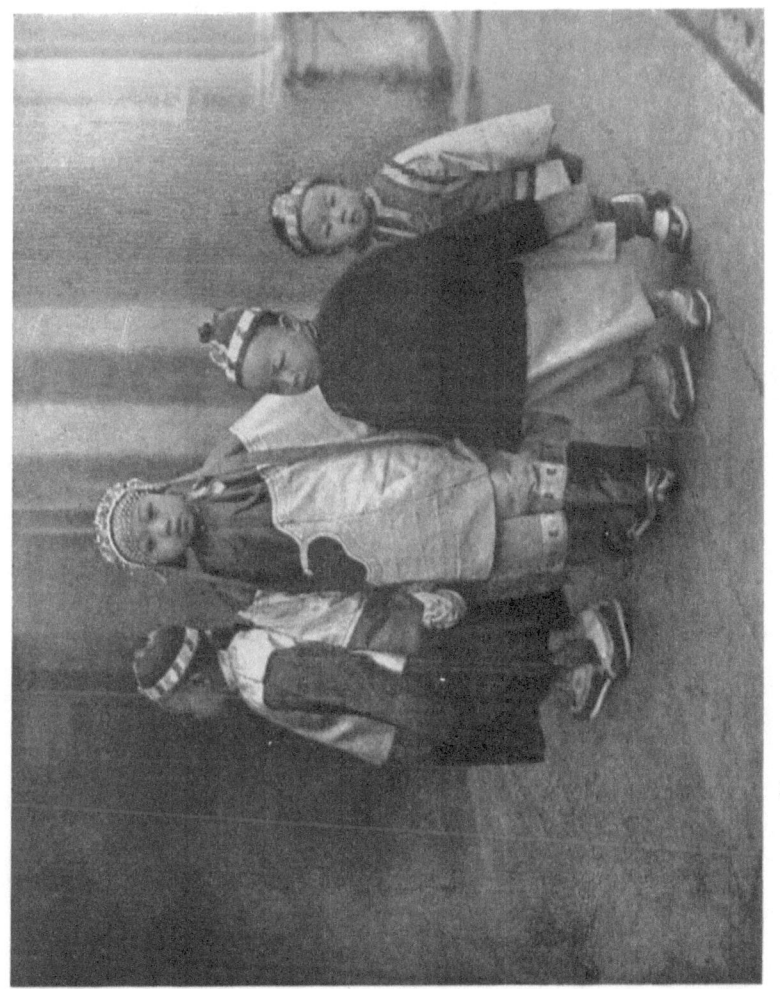

"CHILDREN WERE THE PRIDE, JOY,
BEAUTY AND CHIEF DELIGHT
OF THE QUARTER"

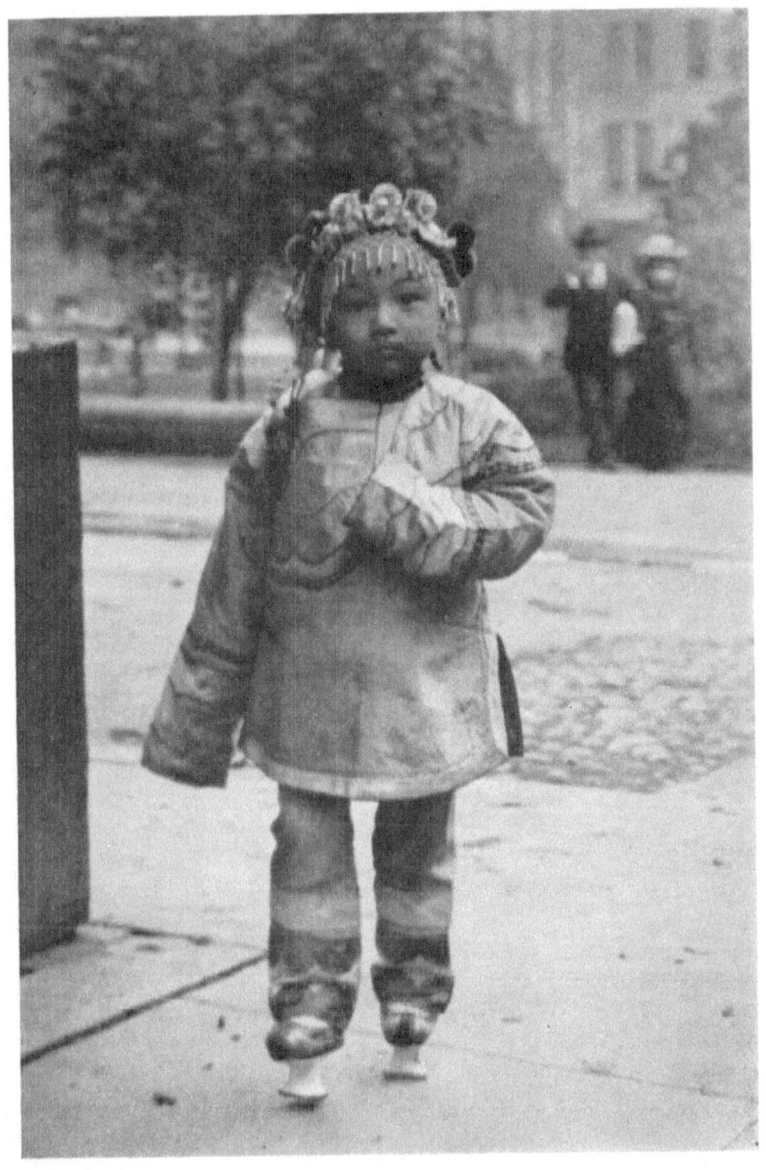

IN HOLIDAY FINERY

"MOTHERS DECKED THEM OUT IN BRIGHTEST SILKS AND CAPS ALL
TINKLING WITH GOLDEN DEVIL-CHASERS"

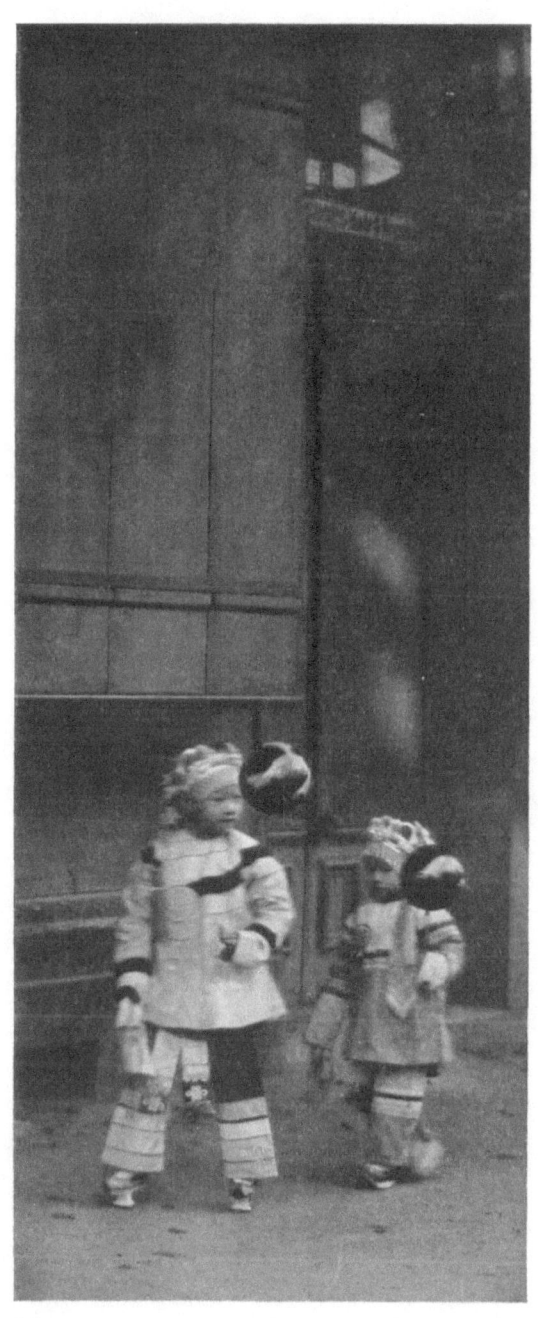

"TINY, YELLOW FLOWERS OF
THE WORLD"

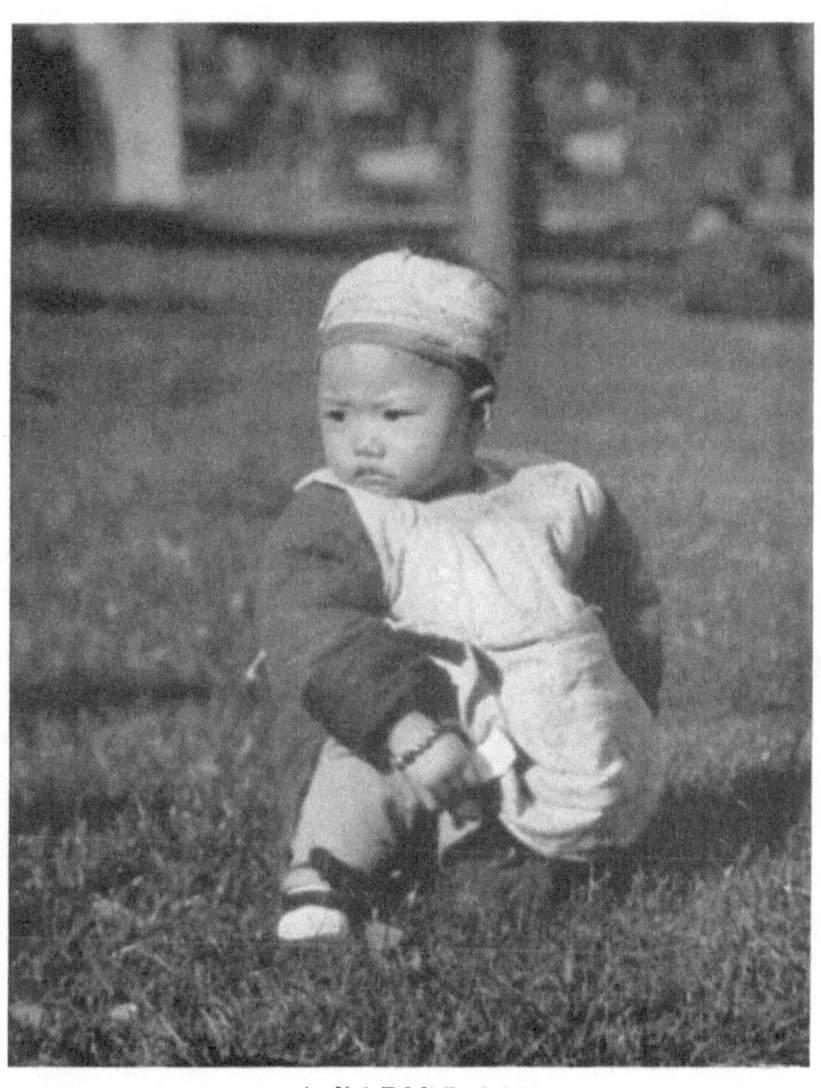

A NATIVE SON

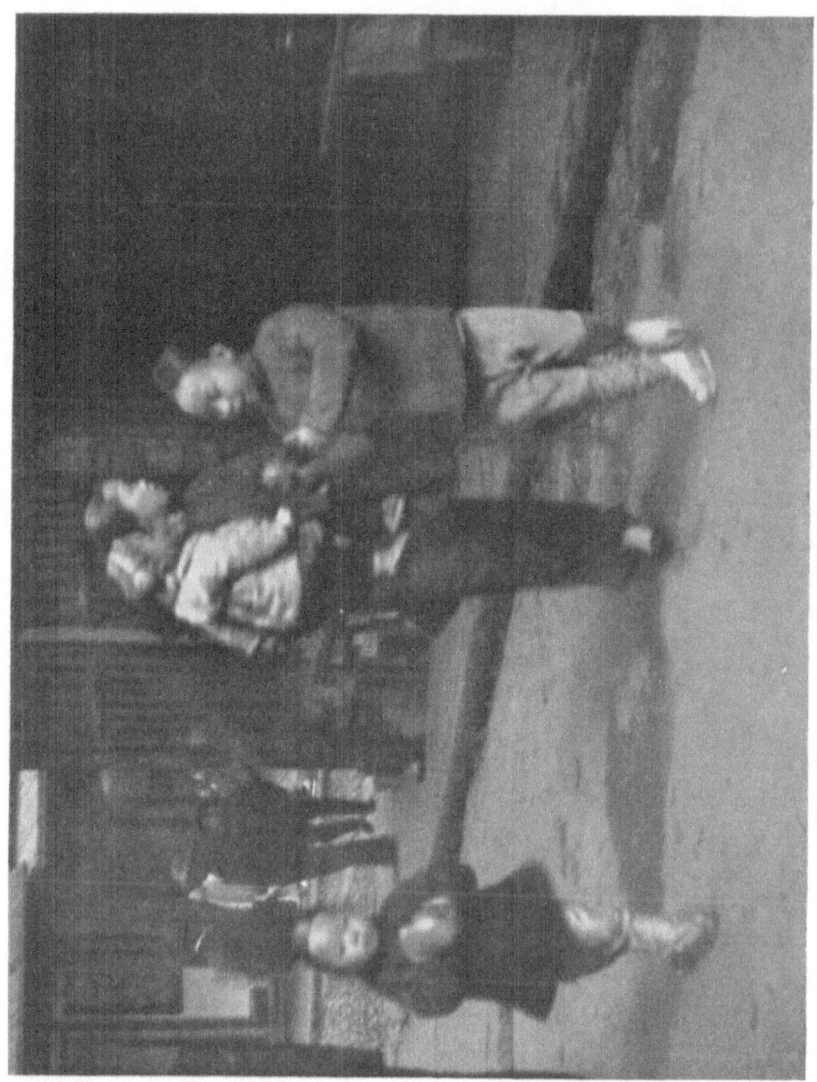

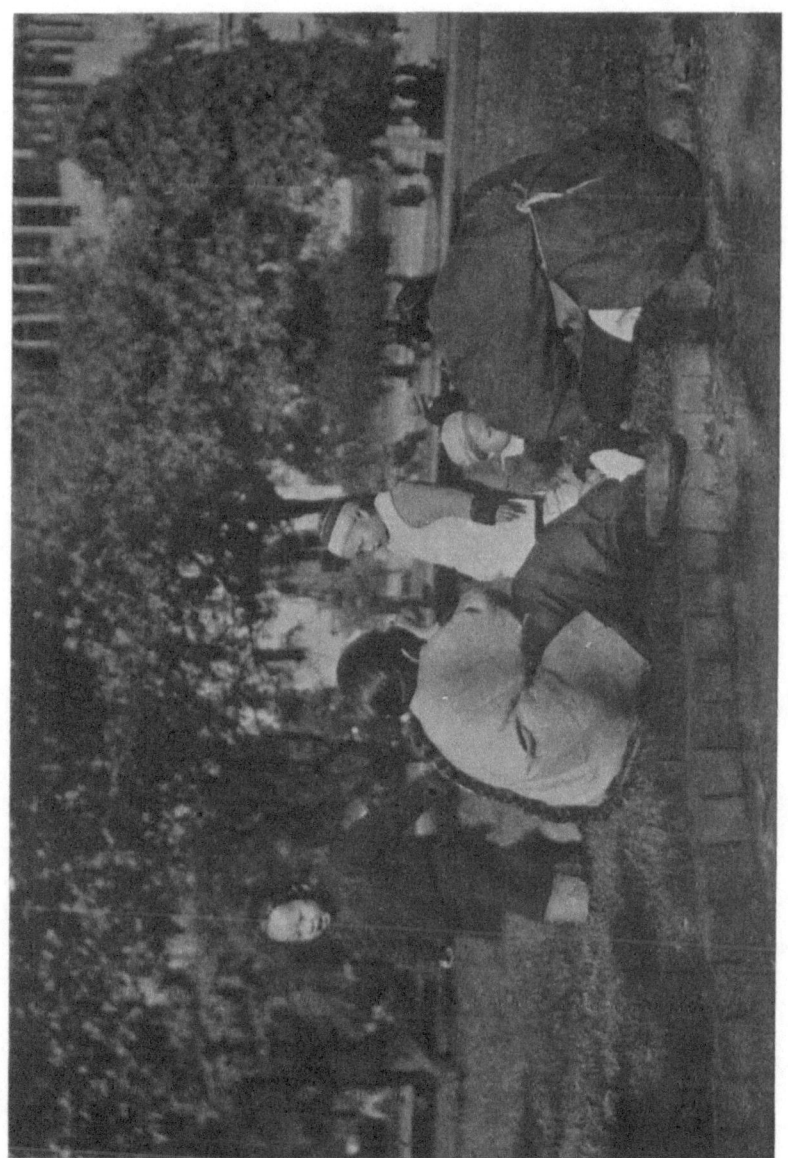

A PICNIC ON PORTSMOUTH SQUARE

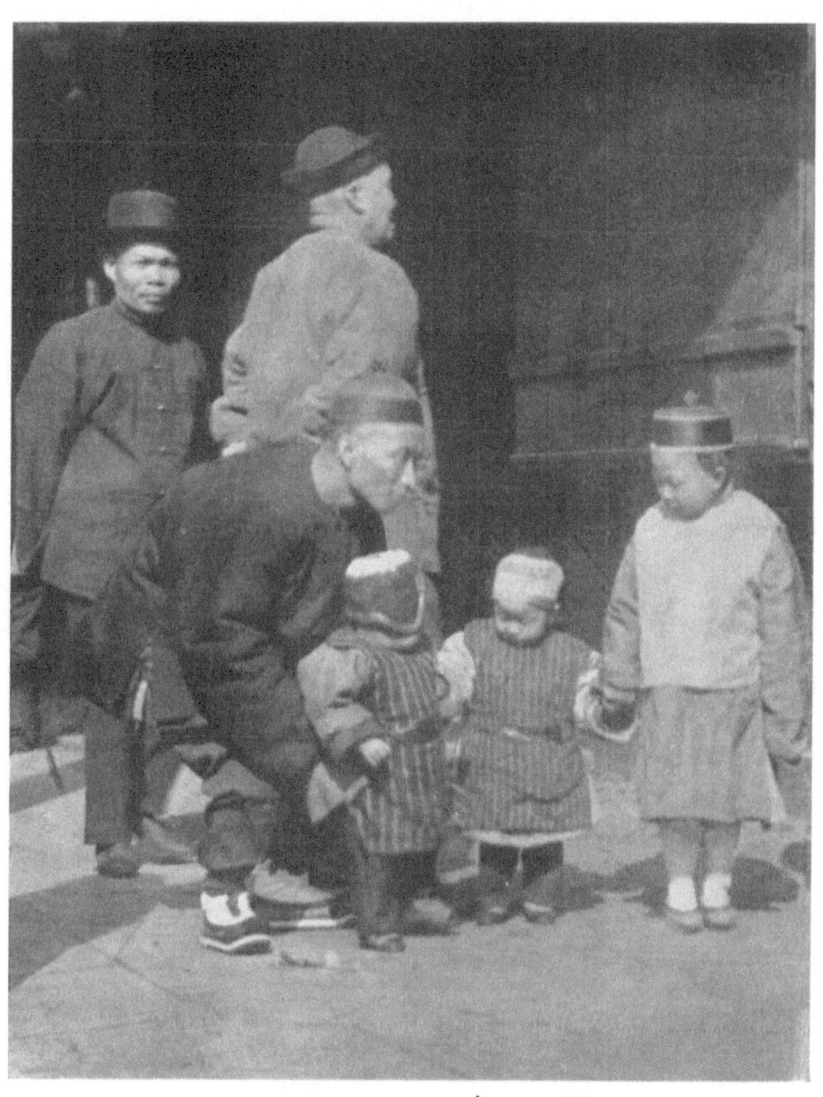

THE CHILDREN'S HOUR

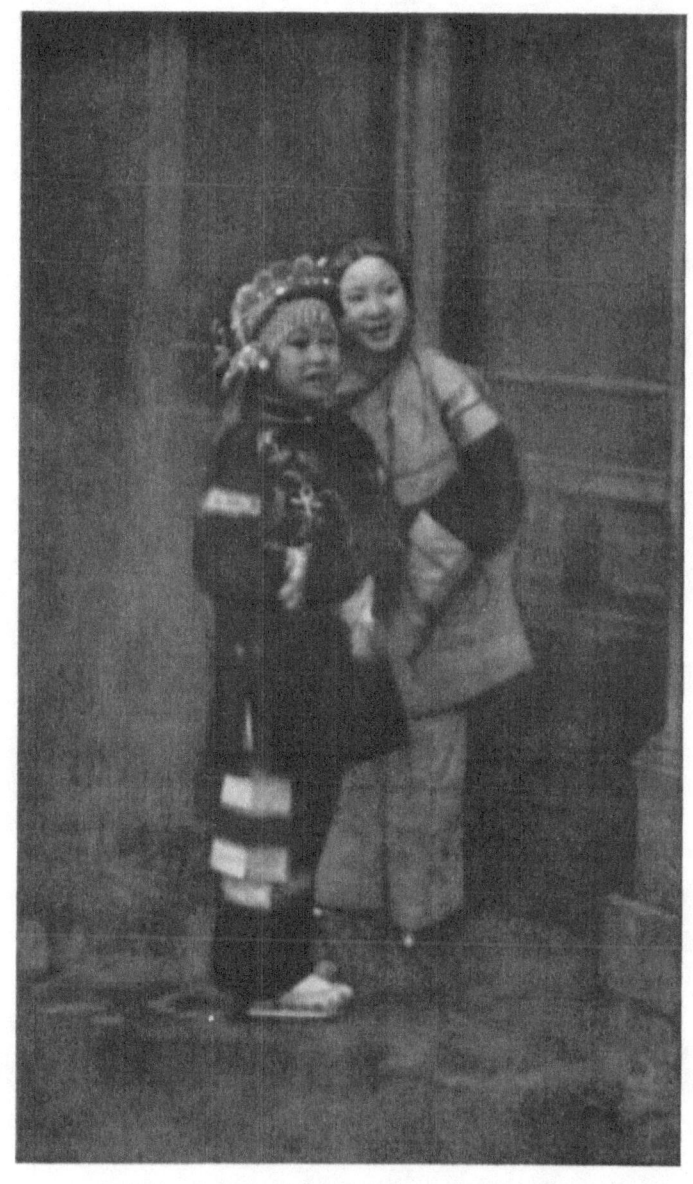

THE DAY OF THE GOOD LADY
FESTIVAL
"THERE CAME A DAY WHEN ALL THE WOMEN, HIGH AND LOW,
HAD FREE RUN OF THE STREETS"

## CHAPTER FIVE

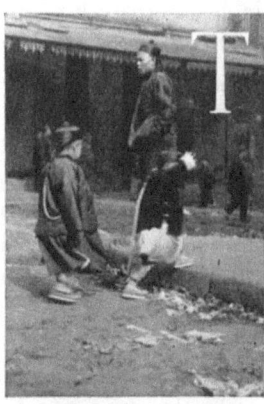

THEY love a fiesta, those Californian Chinese; four or five times a year, some fixed or movable feast brought out everything that was wonderful in the Quarter. Two or three of these holiday occasions linger in memory. On Stockton Street stood the clubhouse of a merchant organization only one whit less powerful than the Six Companies. Once in three years, this club celebrated the glories of its joss and kept open house. The reception was for white and Chinese alike; in this time of peace and good will, they drew no color line. All races mixed in the crowd which packed their rooms to drink tea and scan the innumerable paper altars in honor of this immortal god or that dead hero. Mostly, these altars told, in flimsy paper statuettes and legends on red paper, some tale of old China. There, life size, was the great god, sitting in fearful state and casting forbidding eyes upon the priests who sang before him with many prostrations. About him, stood a dismounted hero in the tasseled and feathered war bonnet of other days; the princess his wife; a horse which was a caricature of an animal in shape and a wonder of art in blended coloring; the seven goddesses, gazing indifferently upon rich offerings of roast pig, incense and fruit.

Near the entrance, in a recess of his own, sat the terrible and luck-bringing joss of the Tong. He is a devil as well as a god; he is beatifically kind and terribly cruel. His image is all white in face and clothing, but his eyes are weeping tears of blood. He is so lucky that just to touch him will make you win at lottery or fan-tan. He was much sought by the thievish; and between festivals the Tong kept him in a burglar proof vault. On this public occasion, when his owners brought him out to bless and help their guests, two white watchmen guarded him with club and gun. No Chinese watchman could be trusted, in face of that awful temptation to win everlasting prosperity at one stroke.

Once, in this week of festivity, they brought him out on the streets. That was on the last night, when the elders of the Tong, in caps and long dress tunics, publicly distributed bread and meat to all the poor of Chinatown, whether white or yellow. Then, priests bore him high in air on their shoulders that he might radiate fortune on the unfortunate.

I remember, too, a certain night in the annual festival of devils, when the orthodox Chinaman purifies his house by a cannonade of firecrackers to keep away the evil spirits for another year. The air, in the Chinese cosmos, is full of devil people; a Chinaman wastes a deal of his time and energy worrying about them. At home, I believe, the very orthodox never make a straight entrance to any building — for devils cannot turn a corner, and a crooked entrance is a safeguard. Behold how superstition yields to convenience! The Chinese of San Francisco had adapted to their uses abandoned American stores and business blocks. It was inconvenient, almost impossible, to screen against devils the entrances of American-built stores. The practical Chinaman, therefore, gave up the doctrine of his creed, and took the more ardently to propitiatory sacrifices and offerings and devil-scaring firecrackers. And at the great devil feast, he fairly outdid himself in casting out all the works of evil, that his house might be clean for another year.

On the night which I am recalling, a certain observation upon the Chinese crystallized in my mind. Out of his mental difference from us, his oblique thinking as contrasted with our straight reasoning, his subtlety as contrasted with our directness, his commercial honesty as contrasted with our comparative commercial dishonor, his gentility as contrasted with our rudeness; further, out of our wholly unnecessary persecution and race hatred, he has come to a superior contempt of us and our ways. Certain broad spirits among them look across the race line and regard us as human beings; certain humble personages among them, such as the old family retainers whom I have mentioned already, develop a curious, dog-like affection. But in the main, they feel a passive contempt. We were to them a medium of commerce when we stopped at the stores to buy; meddlers when we interfered with lotteries, fan-tan games, plague, highbinder wars and other affairs which were none of our business; plain pests when we swept down upon them with uniforms and patrol wagons, but always Things — never persons. You passed them on the streets; they turned out for you; but they glanced at you no more than they glanced at the innumerable sleek cats sunning themselves in the doorways. You might pick a specially beautiful or interesting Chinaman and stare at him all day; he would notice you no more than a post — unless you pulled a camera on him. A Chinese father would, indeed, soften if you stopped to pay court to the baby in his arms; it was too much to expect that he would refuse tribute from anything in the earth below or the air above to the pride of his heart and the hope of his immortal salvation. That, it seemed to me, was the only point at which your Chinese willingly granted intercourse to the despised race.

But on that night, when the punk-sticks and the pocket altars burned at every corner and before every sweetmeat stand, when alleys were canopied over for the use of the priests, when windows glowed soft from the sacrificial lights within; on that night, when horror and mystery held the air — then you paid court to no Chinese baby. Approach him, and his father drew him sharply away; persist, and his bearer would hurry off in a panicky run. Pidgin English brought no answer to your most polite inquiries. The children imitated their elders; the big brother or sister, caring for little Ah Wu or tiny Miss Peach Blossom of the lily feet, scattered fearfully from the foreign touch. We, inferior, uncomprehending, were brothers to the powers of the air. Only this I noticed — your money was still welcome at the stores. Perhaps it was right to take devil tribute.

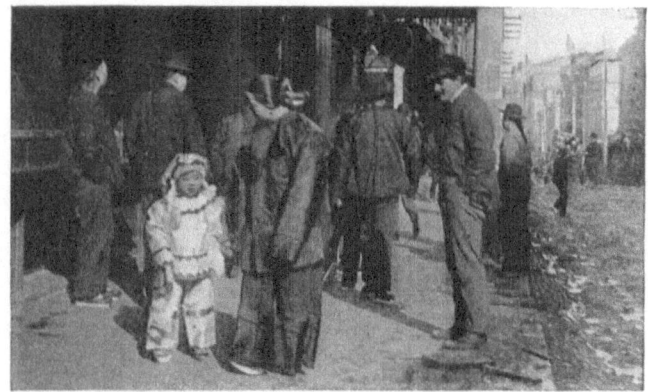

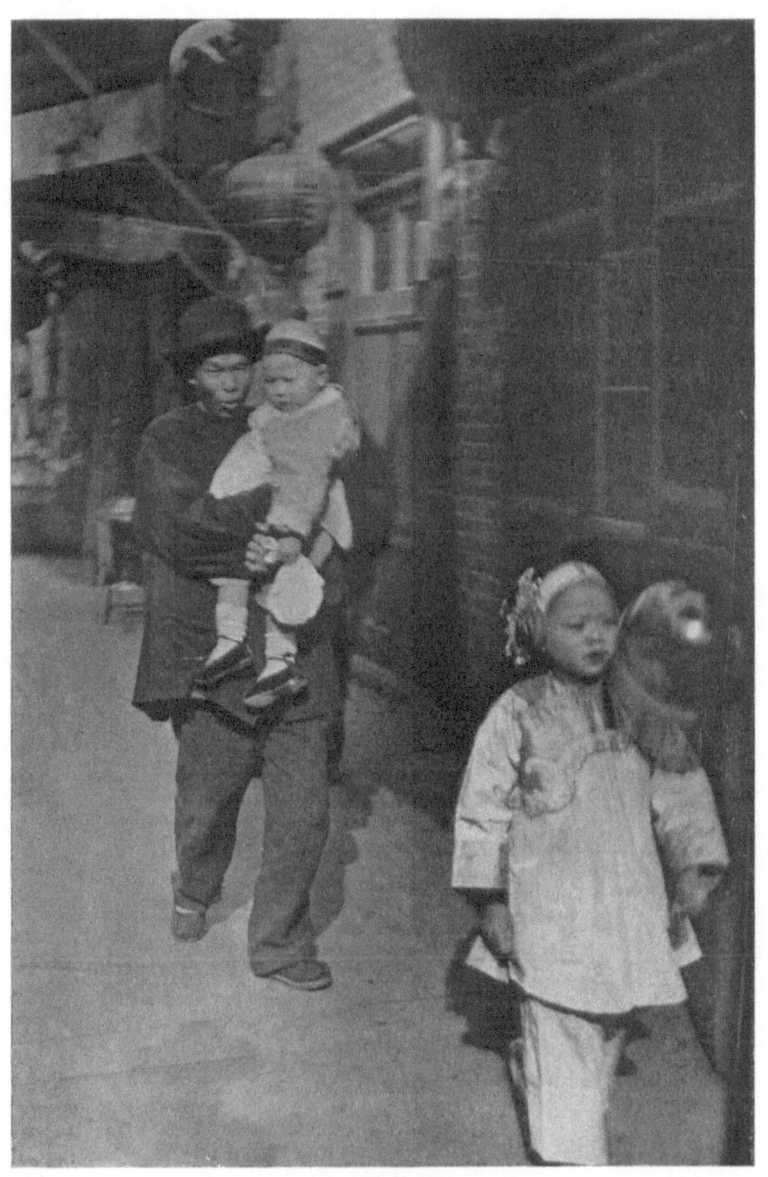

A HOLIDAY VISIT

93

PAYING NEW YEAR'S CALLS

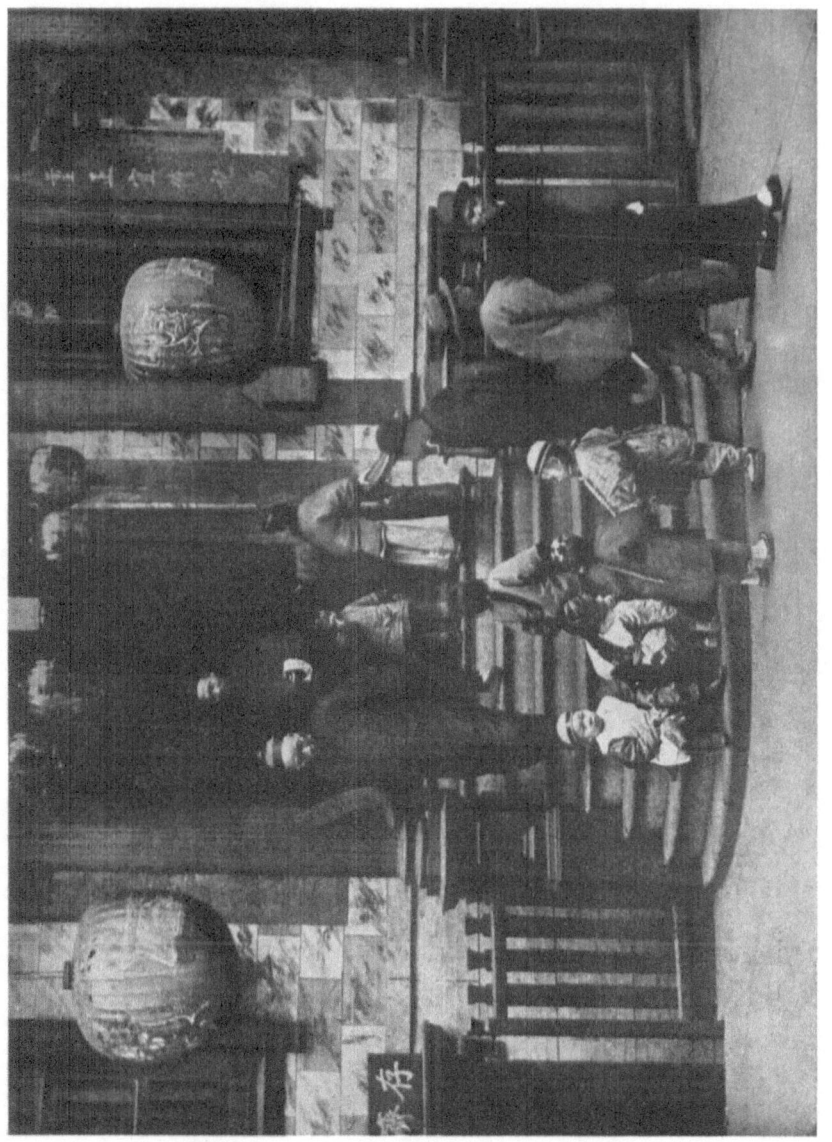

IN FRONT OF THE JOSS HOUSE

"WHERE STRANGE GODS WERE WORSHIPPED BY YOUNG AND OLD"

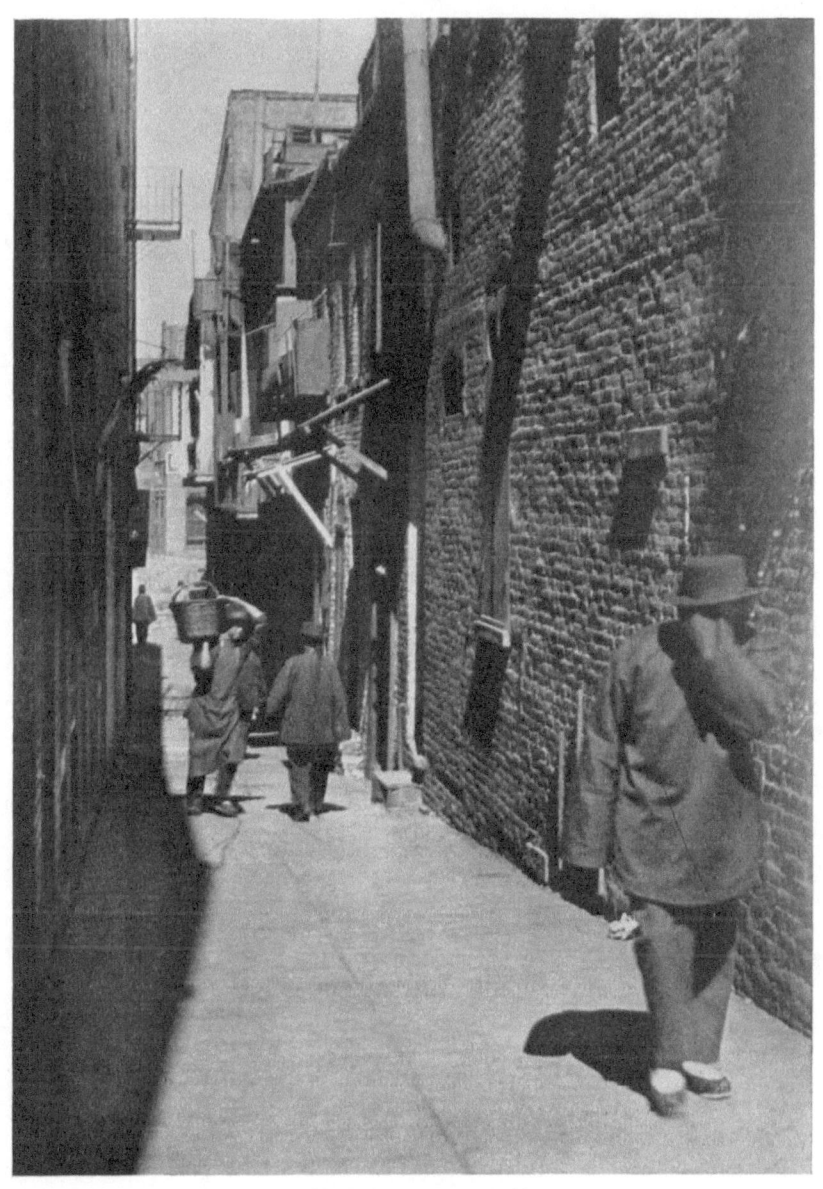

## "NO LIKEE"

"HE WOULD NOTICE YOU NO MORE THAN A POST — UNLESS YOU PULLED A CAMERA ON HIM"

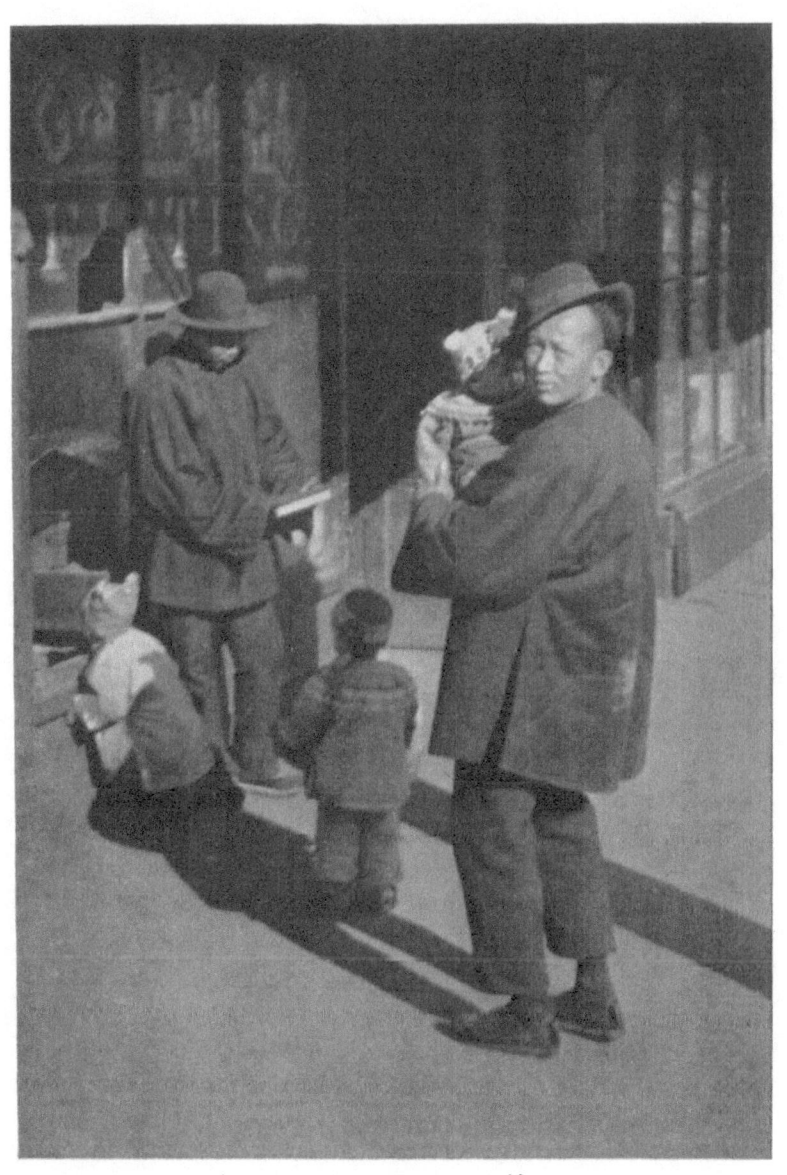

"HE BELONG ME"

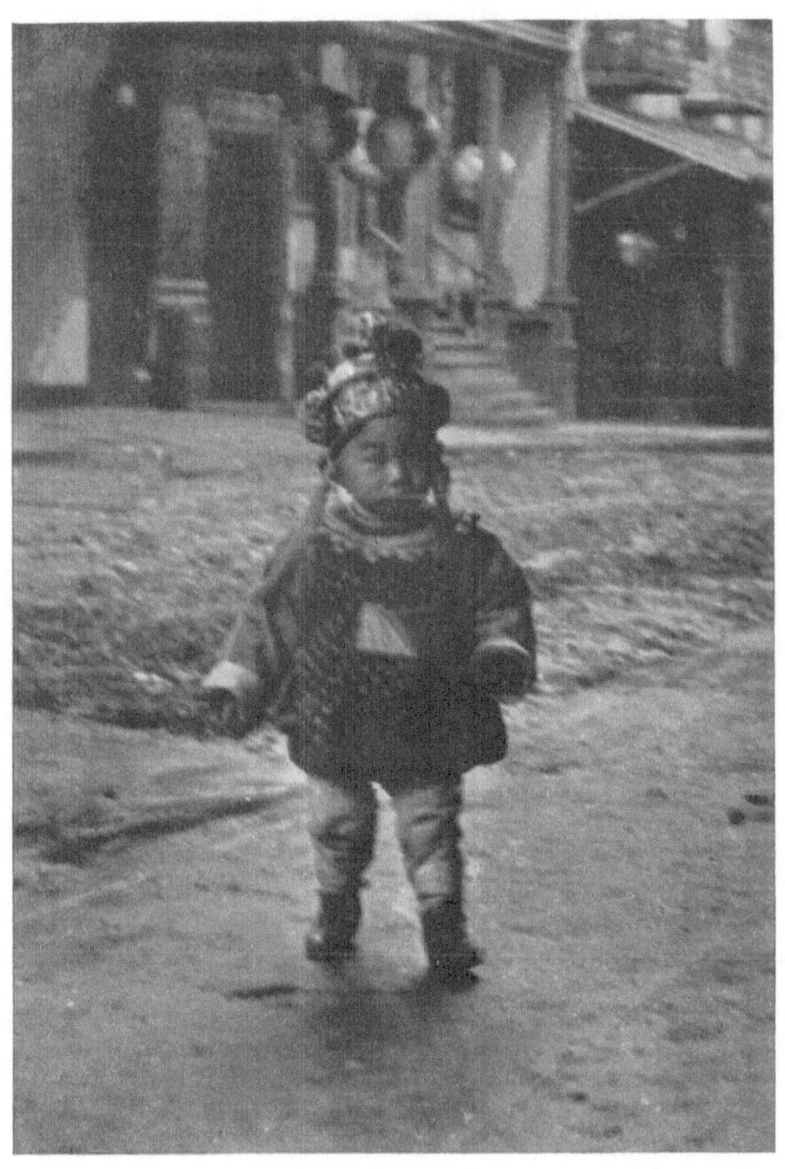

THE FIRST BORN

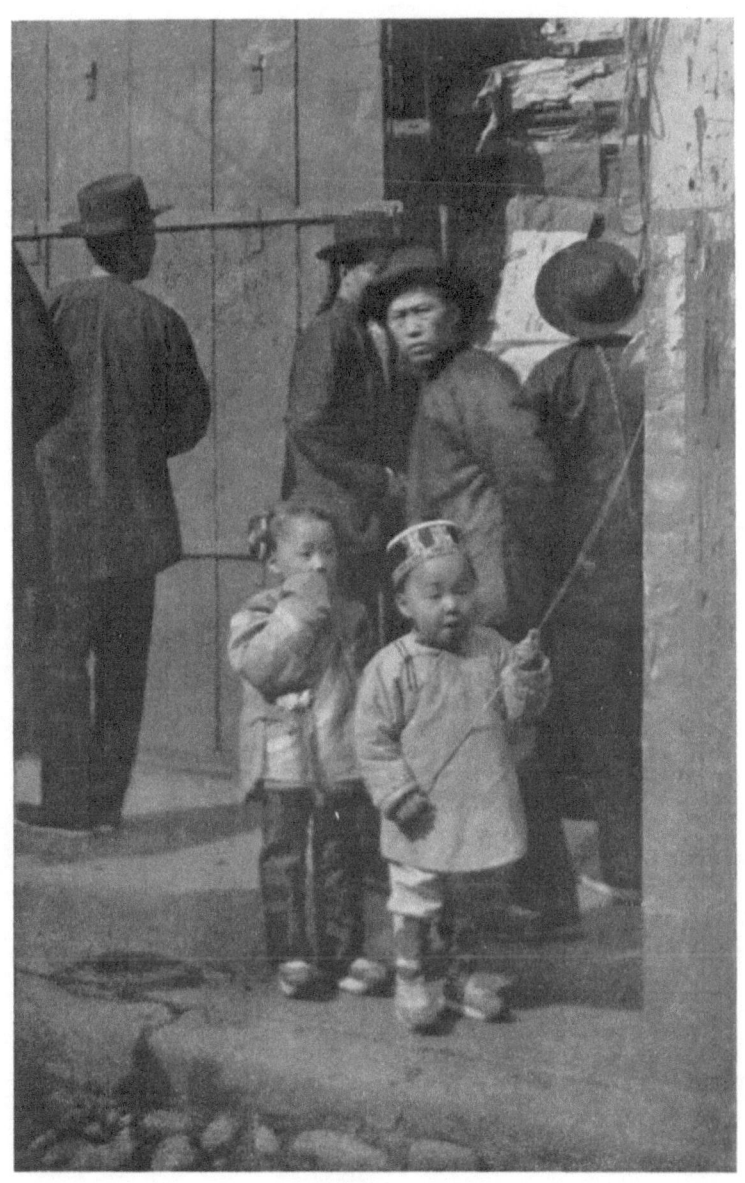

A HOLIDAY

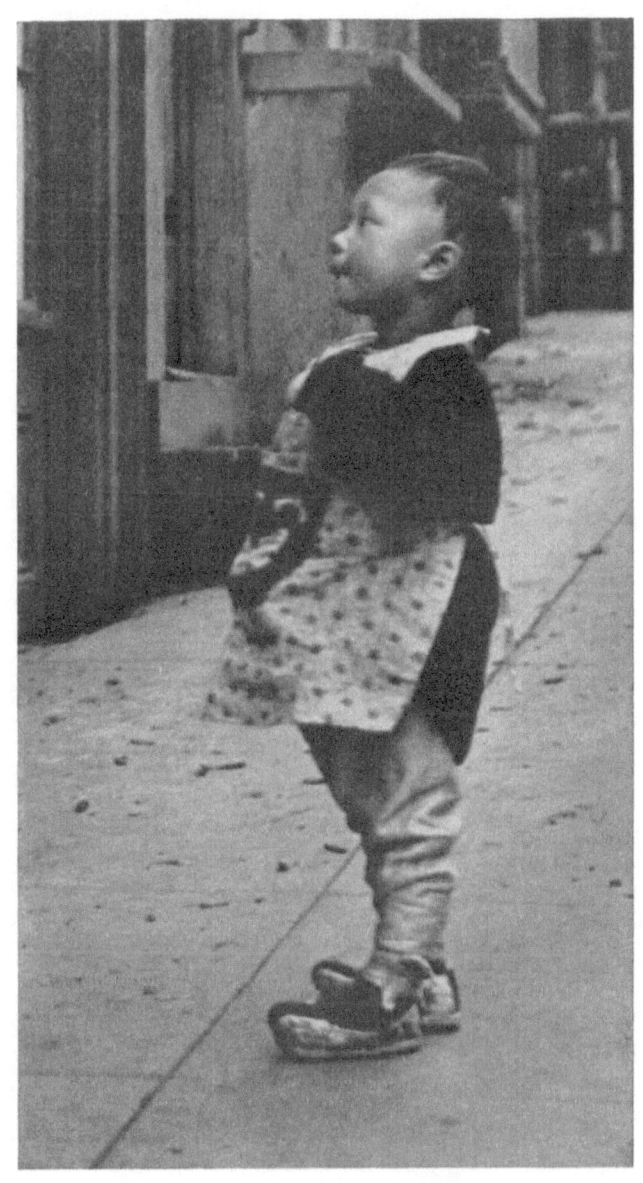

LITTLE AH WU

## CHAPTER SIX

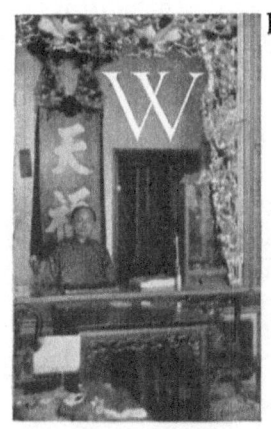

HAT is it which makes one picture of life linger in memory while others, and more marvelous ones, fade out? Vividly I remember a dinner party which I saw that night. Perhaps I had with me a friend, whose identity is the one thing which has gone from me, but whose strong and stimulating pull on my mind lingers on this rise of memory to a permanent thing; perhaps that was one of those nights of youth when the world is right and life dances down before you, and all your powers are multiplied by some golden number of the gods. At any rate this picture remains, while greater and brighter things linger only in blurred outlines.

It was on the top floor of the old Man Far Low Restaurant on Dupont Street, a show place it is true, but also the great café of the rich and dissolute. That floor, running clear through the block, was a succession of private dining rooms, divided

one from the other by carved screens. The guests
sat not on chairs, but upon square stools of teak
wood. From the front apartment, you stepped out
upon a balcony made into a little Chinese garden.
This looked upon the dark stretch of Dupont Street.
At the rear was another balcony, a small, undeco-
rated thing; and from that you saw Portsmouth
Square with its gilded caravel set in memory of
Robert Louis Stevenson, and still further the
golden delights of the great bay. One who came to
enjoy the Man Far Low must buy at least tea and
sweetmeats. The tea, poured from the crack between two bowls, one inverted over the other, was
of a light lemon yellow, and fascinating to the taste.
One ate the sweetmeats — picked ginger, preserved
nuts, plums and citron — from the end of a spindly
tin fork after failing in the effort to manipulate the
ivory chop-sticks. When the guest had finished, the
waiter stood at the head of the stairs and bawled
something in Cantonese. That was the check; the
cashier, sitting in round cap and horn spectacles
at the desk below, knew by it how much to collect.

That night, however, the Chinese occupied it; a
great, expensive dinner was proceeding in the front
apartment. At the biggest table sat a dozen Chinese
men, very dignified as to dress, for they wore the
long, silk tunic of ravishing neutral tint which is
dress coat and frock coat both to a Chinese gentleman. With each man sat his woman — not at the
table, but just behind, so that she had to reach
modestly over his shoulder to get at the viands in
their toy porcelain bowls. When her lord's appetite
failed, she fed him with her plaything hands; when

he wanted a cigarette, she lighted it for him between her own painted lips. One of these women, I remember, had a homely, irregular face, with a broad mouth, but with an illumination and expression in her features exceptional among Chinese women. A soubrette sauciness showed in her every gesture, but you felt that it was a measured impudence which knew its convenient bounds. Musicians, squatted on a woven straw couch in the corner, were playing a moon fiddle, a sam yin and a gong.

Presently, the feast having reached the stage when food is less to the feaster than drink, they began to play "one-two." I must explain that game, so simple and so appealing to the convivial. You challenge a partner. If he accepts, you throw out from your closed hand any number of fingers from one to four and call off in a loud tone of voice the proper number of fingers. He throws out the same number of fingers and calls the number after you. But at last you call out, craftily, any one number, and throw out a different number of fingers. And if, by calling that number after you, he shows that he has failed to watch your hand, he has lost; and he must drink a cup of rice brandy as a forfeit. He who first becomes drunk is "it." It goes faster and faster, until all the table is playing it in pairs. "Sam!" "*Sam!*" "See!" "*See!*" "Yee!" "*Yee!*" "Sam!" "*Sam!*" Then a chorus of Oriental laughter, more crackling and subdued than ours; for the proponent, on "Sam" (three) has thrown forward only two fingers, and the opponent, falling into the trap has thrown out three. So he is caught, and down his throat goes the forfeit.

[ *111* ]

And as they drank and played, and played and drank, something deep below the surface came out in them. Their shouts became squalls; lips drew back from teeth, beady little eyes blazed; their very cheek bones seemed to rise higher on their faces. I thought, as I watched, of wars of the past; these were not refined Cantonese, with a surface gentility and grace in life greater than anything that our masses know; they were those old yellow people with whom our fathers fought before the Caucasus was set as a boundary between the dark race and the light; the hordes of Genghis Khan; the looters of Attila.

The "its" fell out one by one, retired with some dignity to the straw couch and to sleep. She of the saucy, illuminated face crept close to her lord and whispered in his ear — she, like all her kind, was taking the moment of intoxication to ply her business; and the debauch was nearly over. Only when I was out on the street, and purged somewhat from the impression of Tartar fierceness which that game of "one-two" had given me, did this come into my mind: there had been not one unseemly or unlovely act in all that debauch of young bloods and soiled women, not one over-familiar gesture. Tartar though they had shown themselves, they had remained still Chinese gentlemen and Chinese ladies.

These pretty and painted playthings of men furnished a glimpse into Frank Norris's Third Circle, the underworld. We shall never quite understand the Chinese, I suppose; and not the least comprehensible thing about them is the paradox of their ideas and emotions. On the anomalies of Chinese courage, for example, one might write a whole treatise. A Chinese pursued by a mob never fights back. He lies down and takes his beating with his lips closed. If he is able to walk when it is done, he moves away with a fine, gentlemanly scorn for his tormentors. To take another instance; at Steveston, in the mouth of the Frazer River, the white and Indian fisherman struck. The owners, supported by the Canadian militia, decided to man the boats with Oriental cannery laborers. The Japanese jumped at the chance. The Chinese, to a man, refused to go out on the river. They were afraid of it. Yet a Chinese merchant condemned to death by the highbinders, aware that the stroke may come at any time from any alley, walks his accustomed way through the streets without looking to right or left. So it goes, all through their characters. Nothing fits our rules.

By the same token, underneath their essential courtesy, fruit of an old civilization, underneath their absolute commercial honor, runs a hard, wild streak of barbarism, an insensibility in cruelty, which, when roused, is as cold-blooded and unlovely a thing as we know.

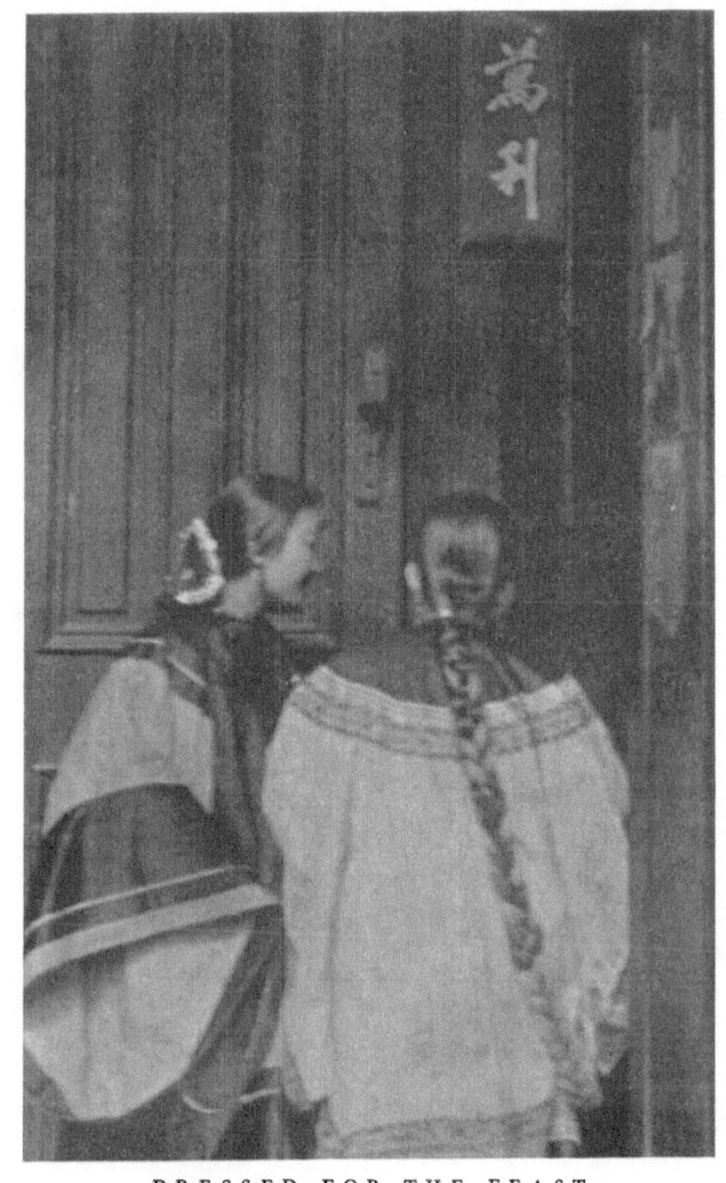

DRESSED FOR THE FEAST

115

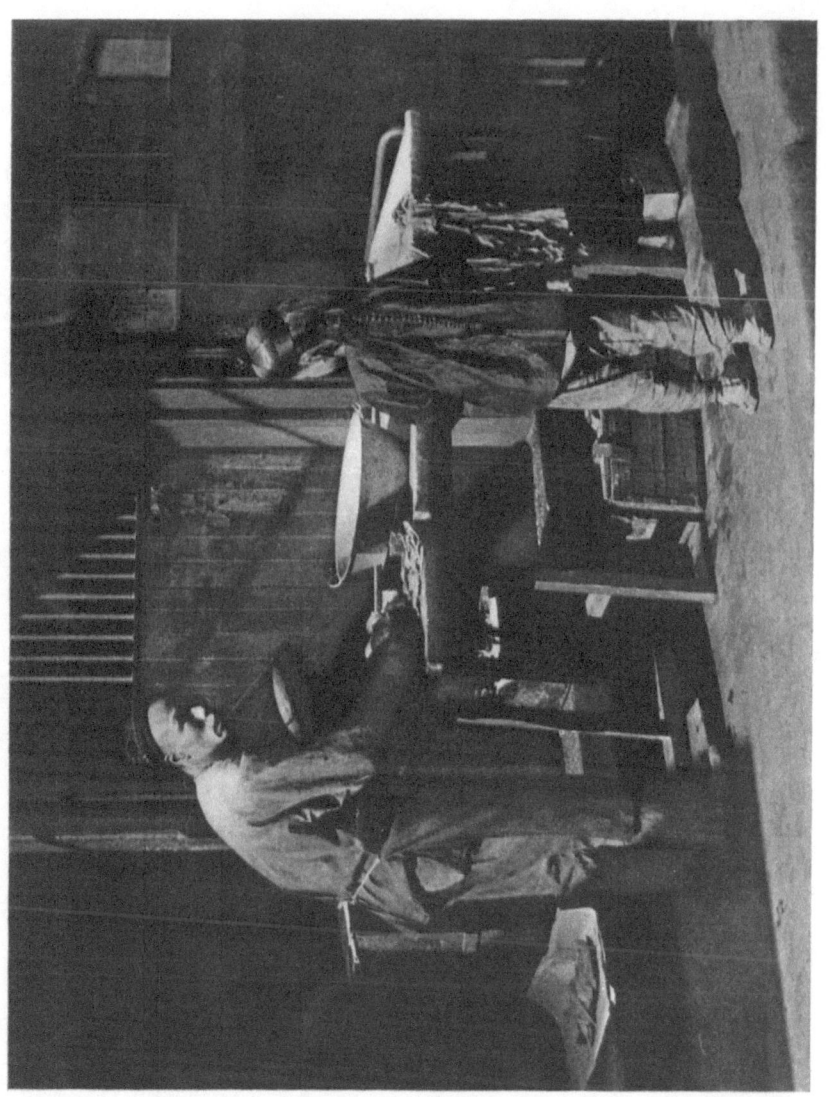

117

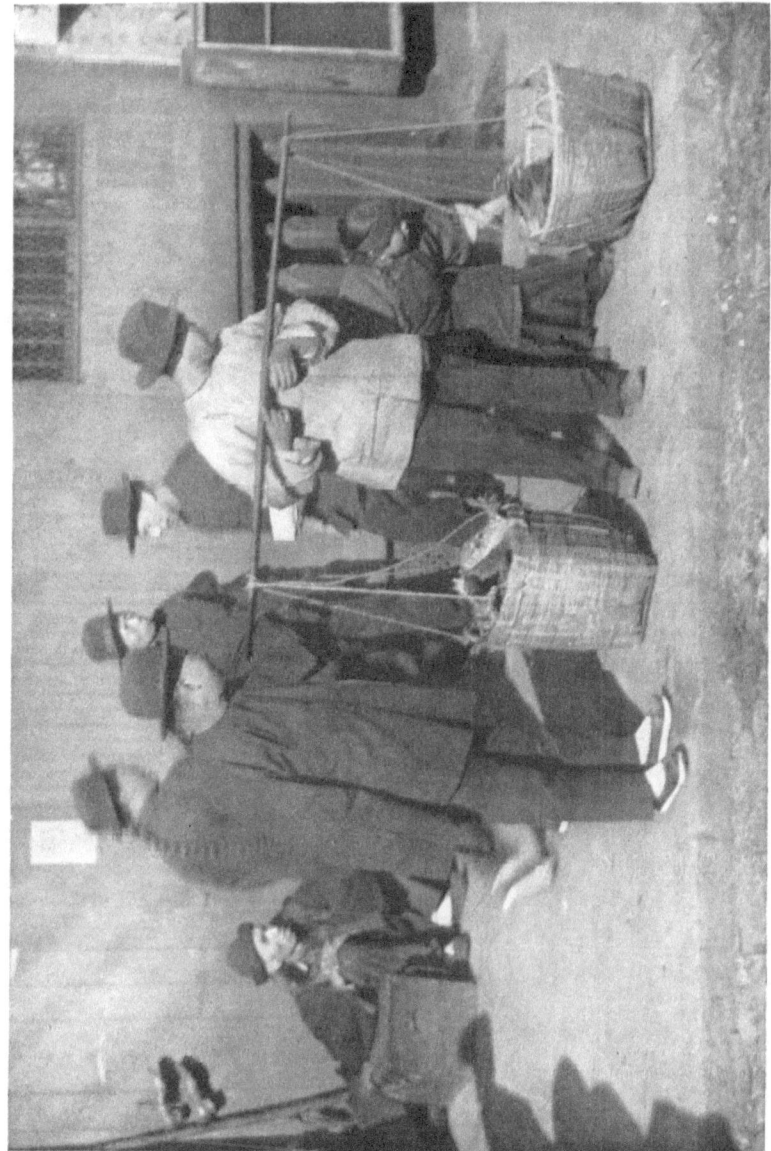

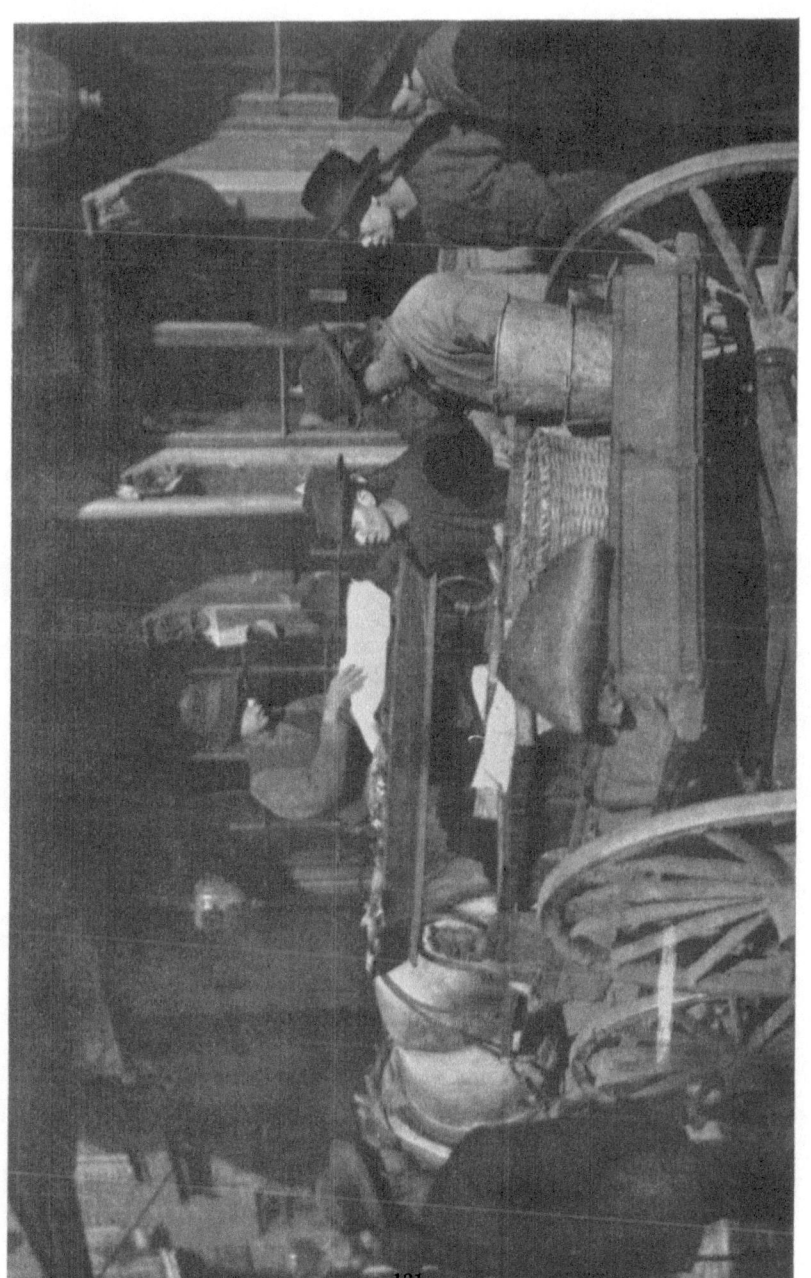

THE FISH PEDDLER

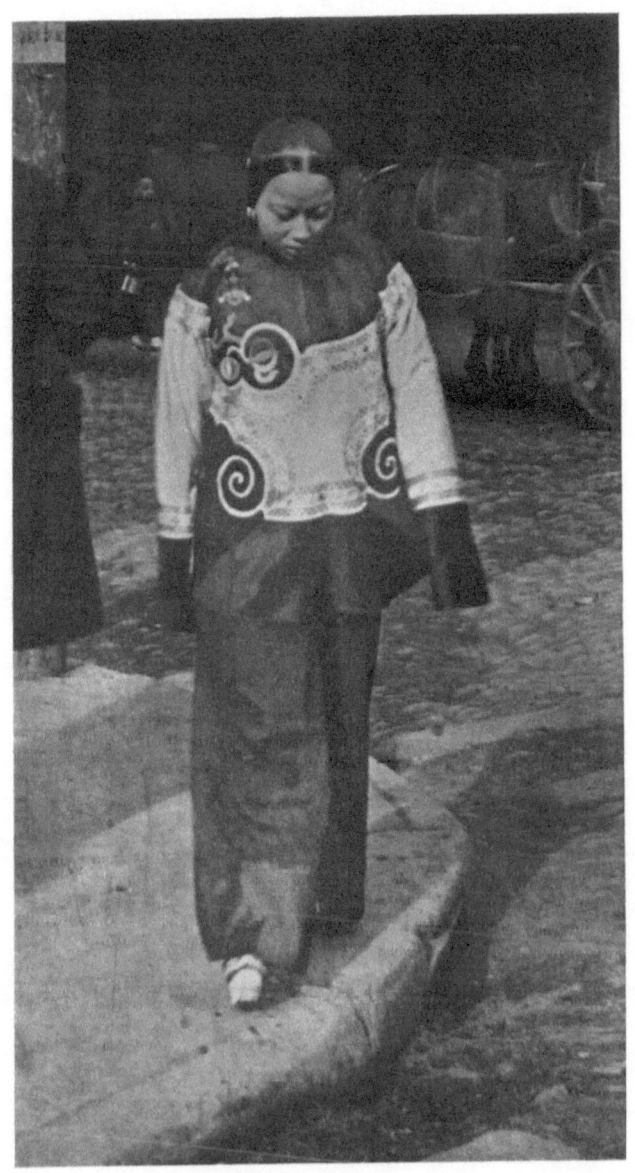

A SLAVE GIRL IN HOLIDAY ATTIRE

123

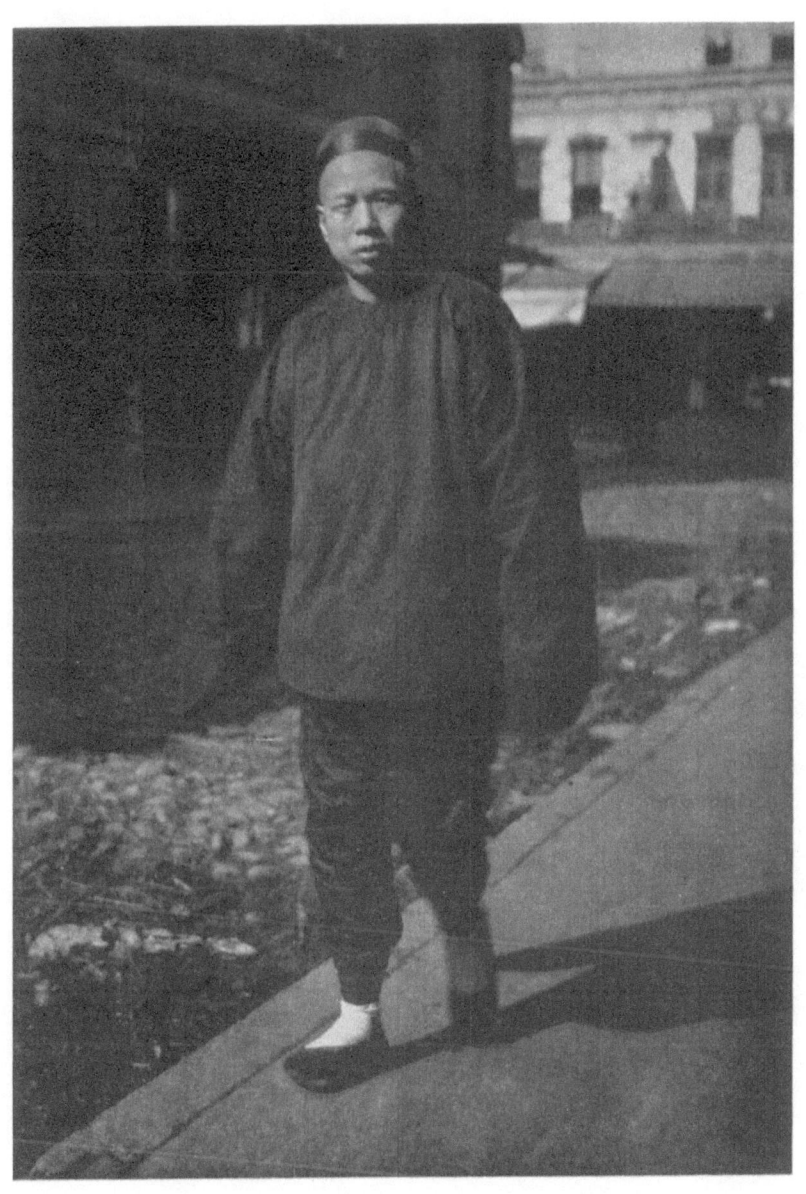

A MERCHANT

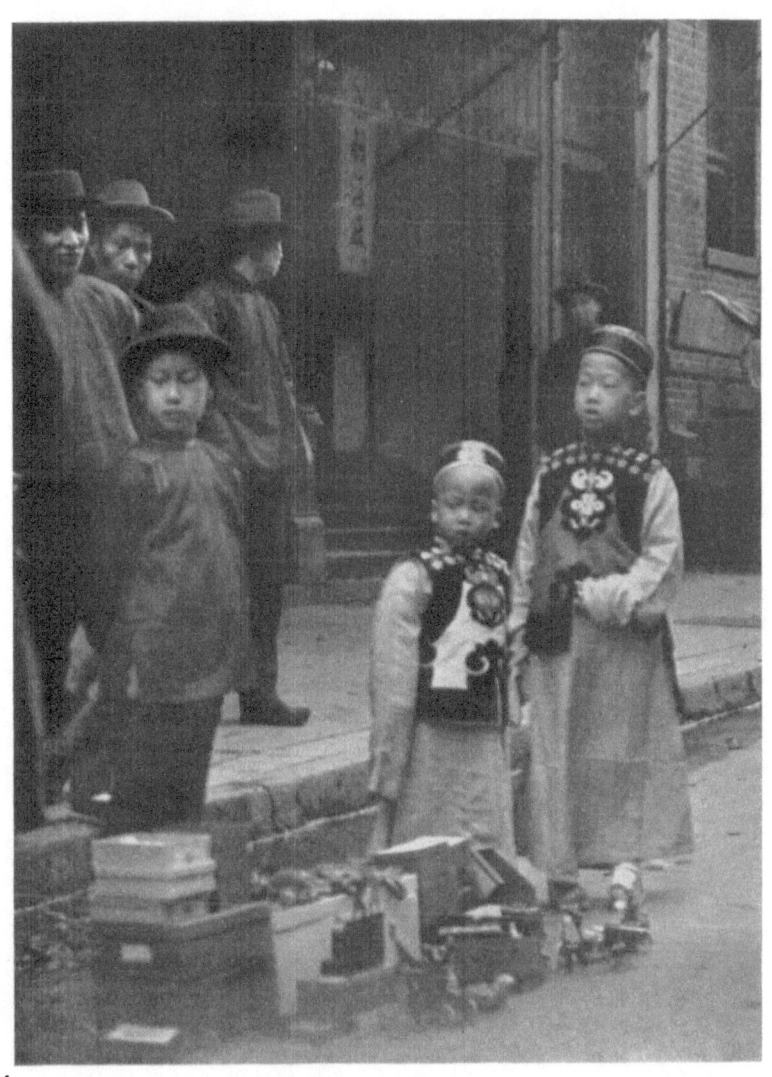

YOUNG ARISTOCRATS

## CHAPTER SEVEN

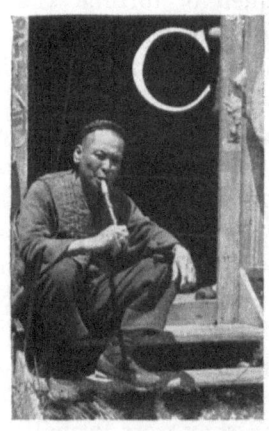

CHINATOWN, the Tenderloin for all the Western Chinese, lived not only by tea and rice and overalls and cigars and tourists, but also by the ministry to dissipation. It had gathered to itself the tough citizens, and especially the gamblers. Gambling is a darling sin to all the race; take his fan-tan counters and his pie-gow blocks away, and he will bet on the number of seeds in an uncut orange. With most, it is a mere diversion. Your efficient, quiet houseboy will go into Chinatown on Saturday night, have his little whirl at fan-tan, smoke, perhaps, his one pipe of opium, and return in the morning none the worse for his social diversion. Others get the passion of it into their blood. One hears continually of this or that Chinese laborer, who, having saved for fifteen years to go back to China and live on his income, has dropped into a fan-tan house on the eve of his departure, lost his whole pile in one night, and returned, with a great surface indifference, to begin a life of service over again. Fat and powerful waxed the keepers of gambling houses. They came to be controlling factors in the vicious side of Chinatown; and they gathered under them all the priests of vice into one alliance of crime and graft. Those who traded in slave girls, those who ran the cheap, internecine politics of the ward, those who lived by blackmail, and especially those gentlemen of fortune known as highbinders, whose reason for being was paid murder, lived and moved in the shadow of the gambling game.

In the age of public exposures, we have discovered that the powers which we pay to keep order and virtue among us and the powers which minister to our dissipation have a mysterious affinity — that the policeman is constitutionally apt to unite himself in a business way with those who live by vice. In this development of civilization we are as children beside the Chinese; and out of this situation grew the highbinders, adventurers in crime. For they were not only criminals; they were formal and recognized agents of justice. Crime and punishment had become tangled and involved beyond any power of ours to separate them and straighten them out. The constituted police of San Francisco struggled with this paradox for a generation long; and, finally, perceiving that the Chinese would settle their own affairs in their own way, gave it up and let the thing go. They kept only such interest in the Quarter — these Caucasian police — as would permit them to gather that rich graft which made a Chinatown beat a step toward fortune.

# ARNOLD GENTHE

The Chinese have a positive talent for organization. They do everything, from running a store to
keeping up public worship, by companies. Your
insignificant Chinese shop-keeper may belong to a
half dozen tight, oath-bound organizations — social,
religious, financial, protective.

I wonder if I can convey the process by which,
in this transplanted Orient, assassins combined with
justice to keep social order? Be it known that the
Chinese has the most haughty contempt for our
law. He seldom appeals to it; when he does, look
out for some deeper plot. Perhaps he is not wholly
in error; he has perceived how easily a clever lawyer
can beat American courts. Aloof from our laws,
then, and still apart from the laws of the Orient,
these perpetual foreigners had to create some system of justice and punishment among themselves.
Of this justice and punishment, the highbinders,
criminals themselves, are also the executioners.

Suppose, then, that you are Wong Kip, Chinese
merchant, and that one steals from you, or commits
the fearful crime of repudiating a just debt. You
do not bother with the American courts. If the
thing is bad enough to warrant the trouble, you or
your Tong-man negotiate with a Bow On or Suey
Sing highbinder. For a sum varying according
to your needs and resources, the hired assassin gets
out his gun.

One night, the man who has injured you walks
fair and straight through the streets of Chinatown;
and a shadow falls in behind him. The shadow
glances right and left to make sure that no white
person is watching. The Chinese spectators —

they do not matter. The shadow walks with his hands tucked, muff fashion, in his long sleeves. They two, avenger and victim paired, reach a dark spot by awning or alley. The shadow creeps up close; his hands fly suddenly apart; a revolver goes off; the sacrifice to justice crumples up on the pavement. The murderer, with the motion of a quarter-back passing the ball, tosses the revolver to another Chinese; it goes on from hand to hand. When the police come at last, the murderer is chattering with the crowd about the body, and that revolver lies in an entrance a half a block away. Twenty Chinese saw it done and know who did it. Will they testify to it in court? Not as they value their lives — not even if they are brothers of the dead.

Only — and here comes the imperfection in justice of this kind — the brothers and Tong comrades of the executed felon often question the verdict and take an appeal. Hiring a highbinder from another Tong, they mark the man who put the wheels of justice into motion — or one of his Tong; it is nearly the same thing — and hold an execution on their own account. This may lead to more reprisals and still more, an endless chain.

Such is the highbinder situation in one of its simplicities. But the further you follow it the more complex it becomes. In the first place, these Chinese toughs, like white toughs, grow restive under peace. When no employment offers, they start trouble among themselves. The Bow Ons and the Suey Sings were eternally straining each at the other. An insult, a quarrel over fan-tan or the price of a slave girl, might set off the mine. There might, too, be a real grievance. It might be a mistress that had deserted her Bow On lover and taken up with a Suey Sing. Here, as elsewhere, women played ducks and drakes with the affairs of men. The offended Suey Sing man would slaughter a Bow On. Not of necessity the offending Bow On; anyone would do who wore the hated badge. The Bow Ons, touched in their soldier pride, would even up the score; the Suey Sings would dispute that the score was even and pick off another Bow On; and the war would begin. Where were our police all this time? "Baffled." The Chinese took care of that. The blue devils who jumped from the noisy wagon would arrest the "suspicious loiterers" whom they found about the corpse, keep them awhile, and let them go for lack of evidence.

Further to complicate the mess, these highbinders had a way of playing foul with their own clients. Constitutional blackmailers, they lived, between wars, on the terror which their name inspired. An order for an assassination might always be turned into blackmail money. The executioner would approach his marked man with a polite, Oriental translation of "Dilly, Dilly, come here and be killed." When the condemned felon had pleaded enough, the executioner would promise to let him go upon payment of a weekly fine. The poor actors in the two theaters, men of no standing whatsoever among their countrymen, suffered terribly from this highbinder game. The slave girls were always falling in love with actors and finding ways to meet them. This offense, in the law of custom, meant death for the actor. The highbinders watched these little games, got evidence, and, by threats of reporting to the legitimate owners of the girls, kept the actors penniless.

A highbinder war tended to go on and ever on. It ended, usually, in a general adjustment brought about by intervention of the Six Companies. Once, a war got beyond all power of this supreme Chinese tribunal in the Occident, and came to trouble the Imperial Master in Peking. The See Yups represent the laboring class, the "unions," in Chinatown, and the Sam Yups the capitalists. In the early nineties, disputes about the price of labor grew into a general strike of all the shoe, overall and cigar operatives. When the strike reached that stage when Occidental strikers began to picket and to loosen entertainment committees, one side or the other called in the high-binders. So wide were the interests involved, so bitter were both the Sams and Sees, that this became a general war, with weekly murders in sheaves of twos and threes. It lasted a year, it sent Chinese merchants into bankruptcy by the score, and it paralyzed all industries except the tourist trade. Its climax came when the highbinders lined up in opposite doorways of Ross Alley, the narrow, over-hung street of the gamblers, and fought until the police reserves charged in between.

At about the same critical period in this war, the See Yups bagged a general. "Little Pete," Chinese millionaire, gambler and man of affairs, had been lord of that little parish. A mere coolie in the begin-ning, he had the golden touch; he made everything pay. He formed a kind of gambling trust in the

[ 134 ]

Quarter, and went out after the Caucasian racing game. He had played at Chinese gambling like Riley Grannan — cold, calculating, without excitement, making the real gambler pay. Just so he played the races, until he had mastered that game and was ready to corrupt it — if it had been possible to corrupt Californian racing. Only when a great scandal broke out in the affairs of the California Jockey Club did the whites discover that a system of pulling horses and permitting "long shots" to win, a system which had been suspected for some time, was conceived and conducted solely by "Little Pete."

Little Pete was a Sam Yup. The See Yups, whose paid highbinders were running behind the score, put a heavy price on the head of this prominent citizen. He sat one afternoon in a barber's chair, having his ears scraped. Two bullets, fired through the open door, caught him in the back and finished him.

His funeral was the greatest public ceremonial that Chinatown ever saw. Echoes from its gongs reached the Chinese Empire. The Consul General got orders to make this foolishness stop. He failed; the war, the state of bankruptcy, went on. The Minister removed him. His successor had no more luck. Finally, the Minister put in Ho Yow, Oxford graduate, brother-in-law of Wu Ting Fang, member of a progressive family, a man who understood the whites and the Chinese alike.

Ho Yow studied the situation and sent representations to China. Suddenly, in scattered districts of Canton, certain innocent persons found themselves under arrest. These were the relatives, even to the third degree, of the men responsible for this war in San Francisco. He served notice on See Yups and Sam Yups alike that any more murders in Chinatown would be avenged upon the persons of these Cantonese relatives. This ended the war with a bang; before the Consul General and the Six Companies, capital and labor made peace. This heroic measure discouraged, temporarily, the high-binder industry. The threat of arrests in China, shaken at the Tongs, has more than once been a restorative of order.

THE STREET OF THE GAMBLERS [BY DAY]

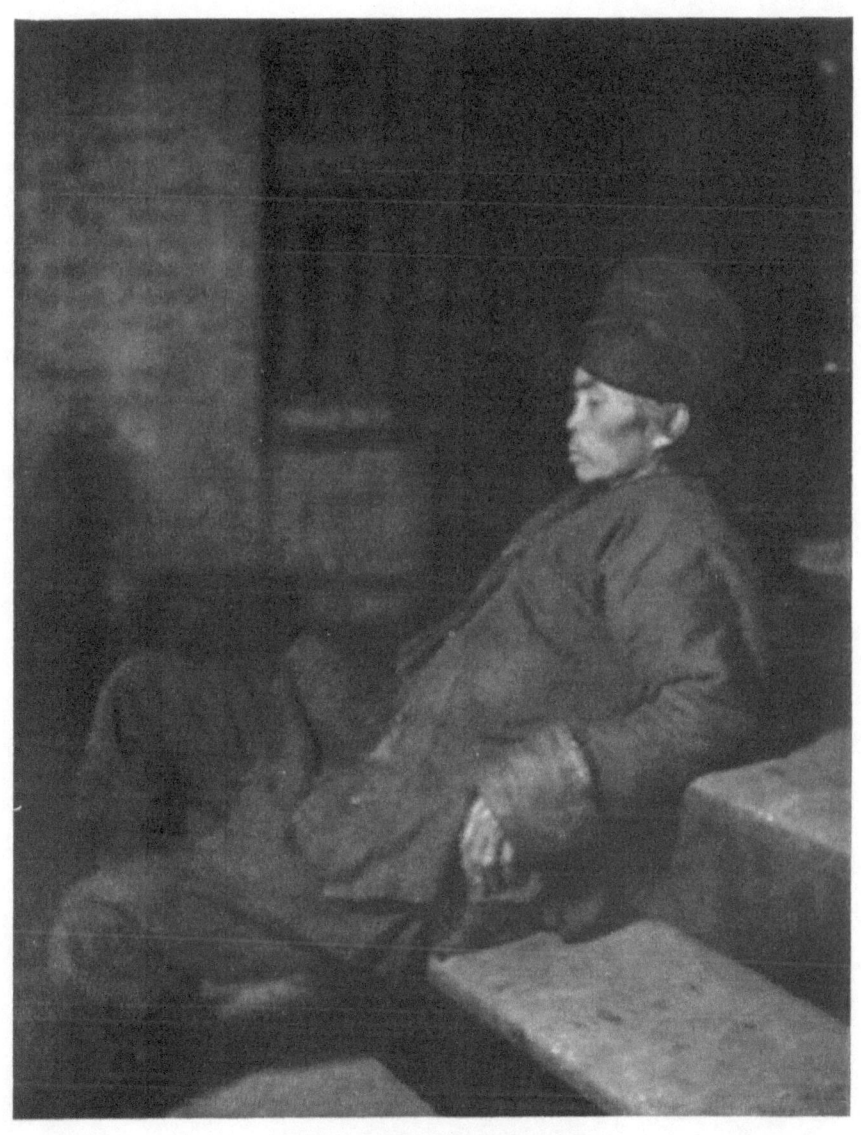

THE OPIUM FIEND

AS THE TOWN DRUNKARDS TO AN AMERICAN COMMUNITY, SO WERE THESE
CREEPING, FLABBY SLAVES OF OPIUM TO CHINATOWN

141

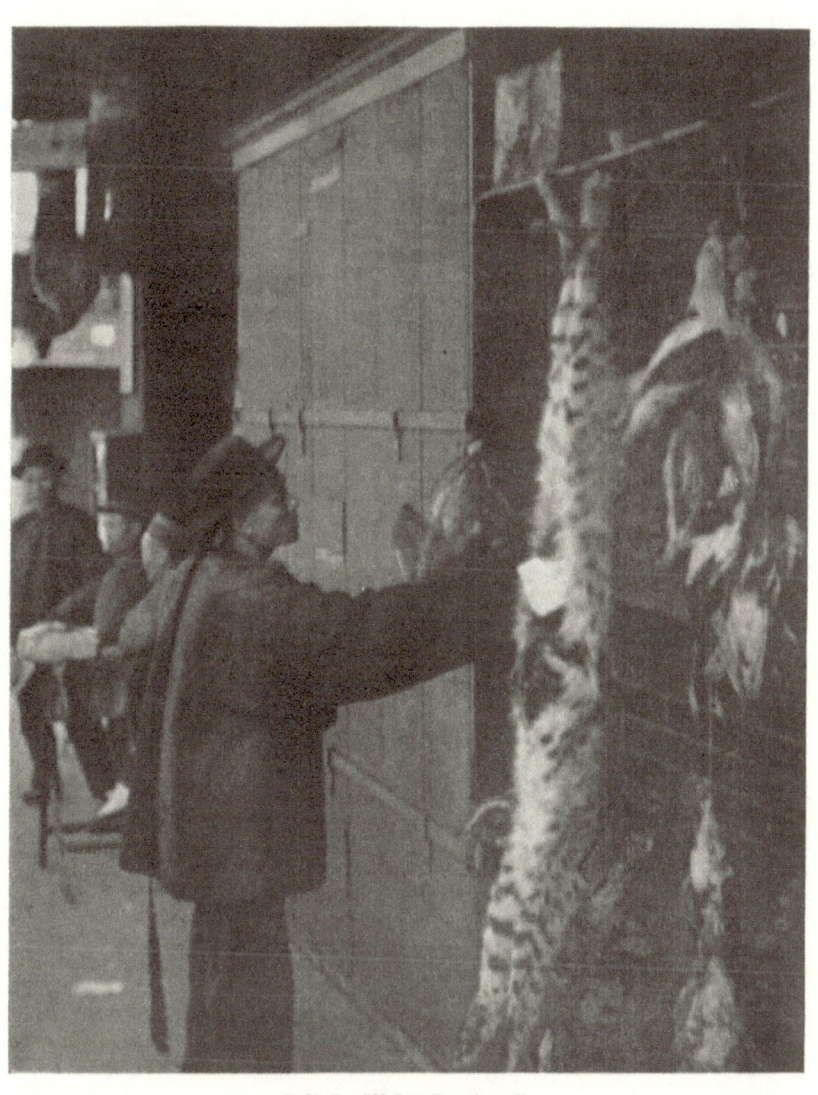

THE WILD CAT

[FOR THE HIGHBINDER'S FEAST OF THE UNCOOKED MEAT]

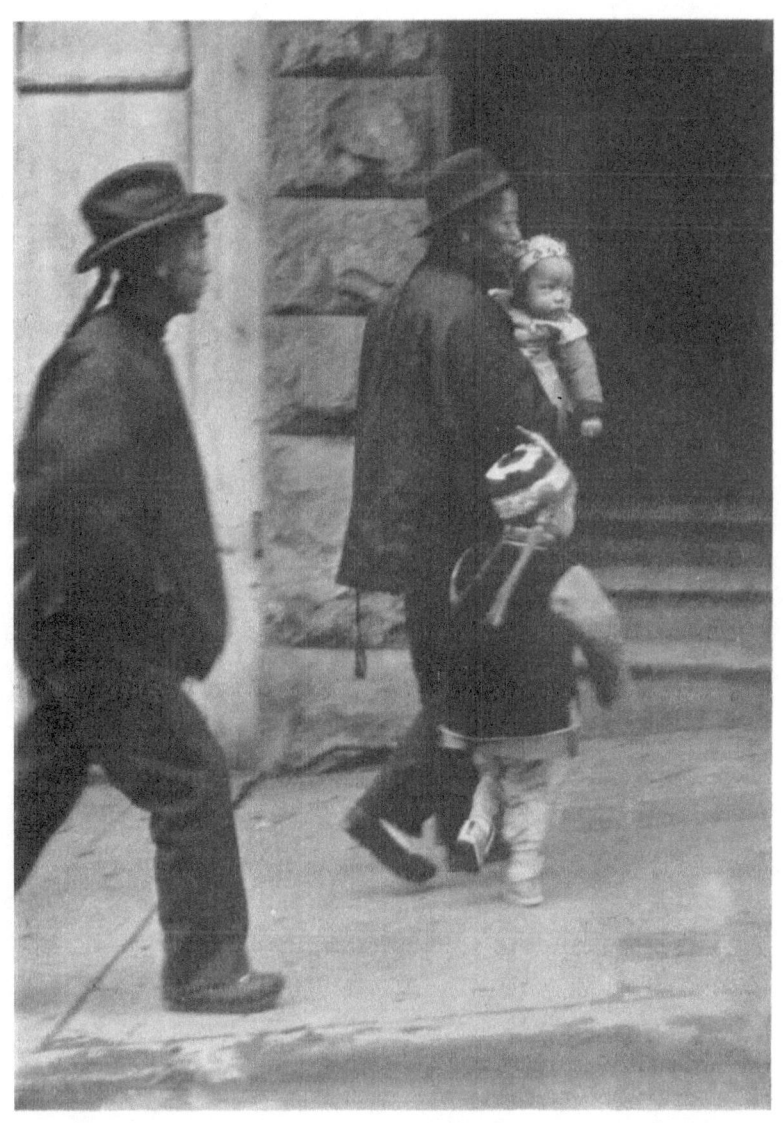

DRESSED FOR A VISIT

145

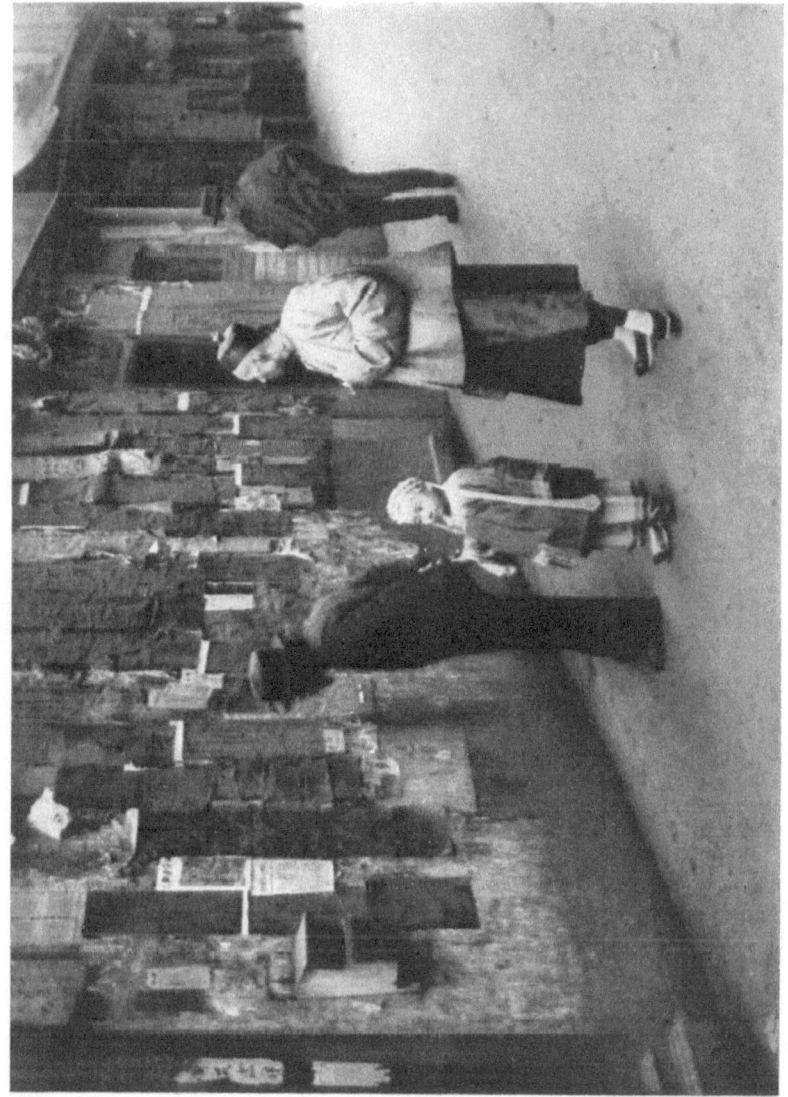

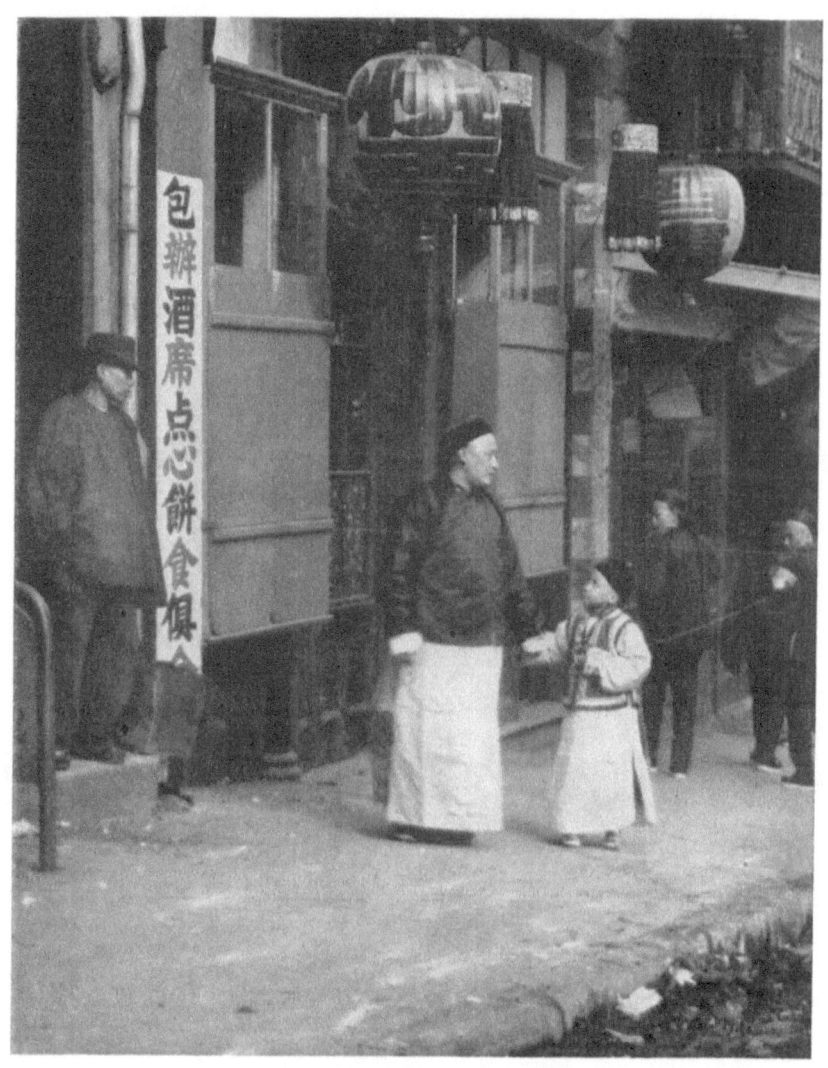

A FAMILY FROM THE CONSULATE

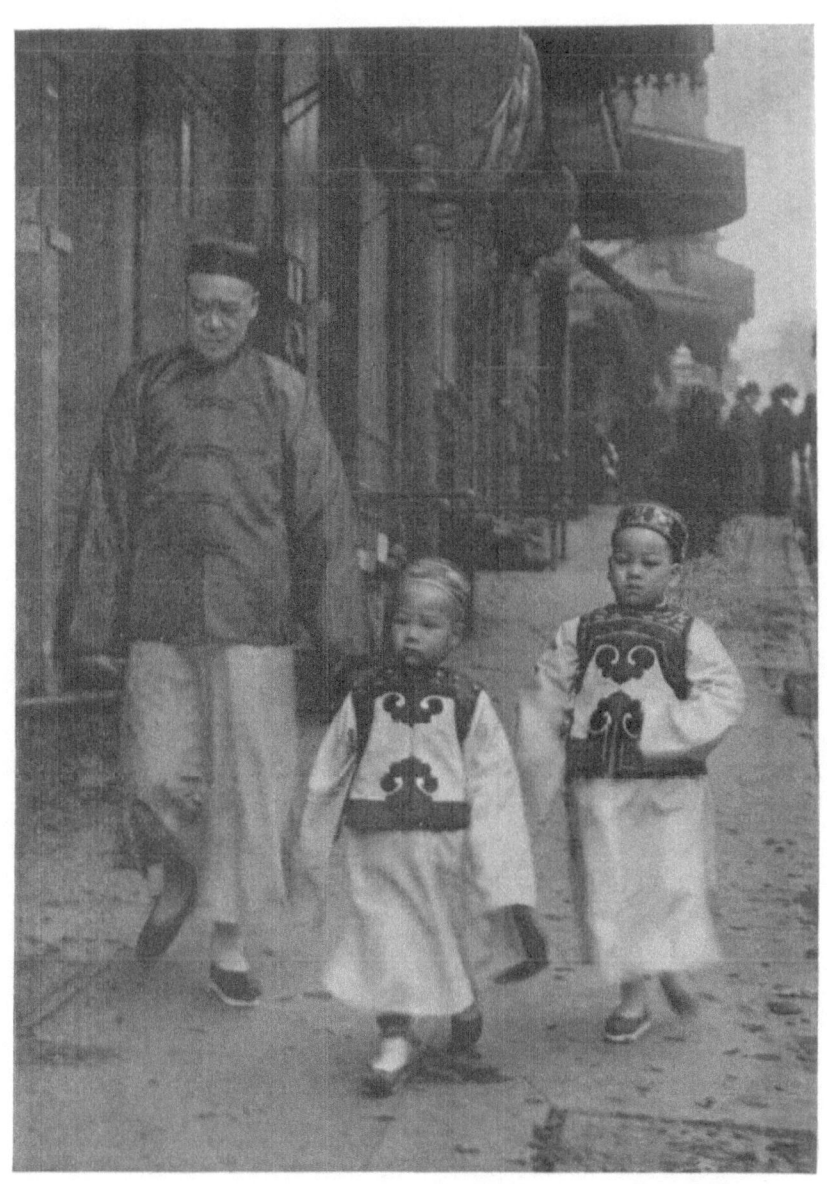

CHILDREN OF HIGH CLASS

## CHAPTER EIGHT

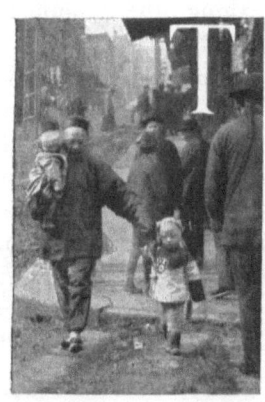

THE underground passages of Chinatown have appealed mightily to the imagination of melo-dramatists, authors of sensational tales, writers for the Eastern press, and others who guide and stimulate the popular imagination. Although some declare them a myth, those passageways of the Third Circle really did exist at one time. Their end antedated the great fire. In the late nineties, a Board of Health, appointed by the last honest municipal government which the old city knew, forestalled epidemics by going through the Quarter with warrant and deputy. Against the diplomacies and concealments of the Chinese, the inspectors closed up cellar after cellar, filled in passage after passage. A few, effectually hidden from that Board of Health or restored later, remained to the end. Still those who knew old Chinatown marveled, when they looked into the gaping cellars left by the fire, to see how little of this mole-work remained.

# OLD CHINATOWN

So wide was this maze, in earlier days, that a
Chinese who knew his way might travel by it from
almost any point in Chinatown to almost any other.
A reporter who held the confidence of the Chinese
has told me how he subnavigated the Quarter during
the quarantine of 1901. The Federal doctors, sus-
pecting bubonic plague, had drawn a line tight about
Chinatown; and, since Federal and not municipal
authorities were doing this thing, the prohibition
against passing the lines was absolute.

A Chinaman, caught outside himself, said to this
reporter: "I take you." They entered the little
den of a white cobbler in California Street. The
cobbler, after a whispered exchange of words,
opened a trap door under his counter. The Chinese
guide, crouching in the shadow, lighted a red paper
lantern; and down a ten-foot ladder they went.
The rest was a bewilderment of knife-edge passageways, stoops, ladders; sudden encounters with
closed doors, from behind which came murmurs of
a mysterious life within; glimpses of other pedes-
trians in those underground streets. Once, they
passed through a moldy lodging house, its walls
dripping with exhalations of the earth, its day-shift
of inmates peering out at them in wonder; once
they came upon a latticed window, strangely futile
in this unlighted world, through which the reporter
saw slatternly women working with something on
the floor — doubtless they were rolling, for warmed-
over consumption, the scrapings of opium pipes.
Once, he thought he heard the sound of moaning.
Rumors of plague were in the air. It came to him
that this might be some one sick unto death with it.

ARNOLD GENTHE

The sense of darkness and confinement made the thought of contagion by Black Death doubly terrible; it was as though he were shut in a dungeon alone with a specter.

They came at last square up against a rough wooden wall. The guide fumbled and scratched and a panel slid back. A drop of three feet brought them into a cellar; from there they walked out of a Chinese grocery store into the full daylight of the Quarter. When the reporter had looked about to his satisfaction, the guide said: "You go back notha' way." Starting from a lodging house next door to the grocery, they traversed more drops and rises, dark passages, hidden apartments, and came out in a cellar of the Latin quarter. They had walked all the way under Chinatown.

Another man has told me how he rambled through some of these passages with a Chinese acquaintance — this was a mere visit of curiosity. When, bewildered and utterly lost, he declared that he had had enough of foul air and suggestion of mystery, his guide mounted a ladder and scratched at a trap door. It opened; and they were in the kitchen of the Jackson Street Chinese Theater, with the gongs of a Chinese orchestra clanging on the stage above their heads.

The exchange of opium, smuggled in from Pacific ships by bay pirates; the heartless slave trade; the preparation of bodies for convenient return to their ancestral grave mounds; the hidden revenges of the highbinders — all went on in these catacombs, twenty feet below the pavement of Dupont and Washington Streets.

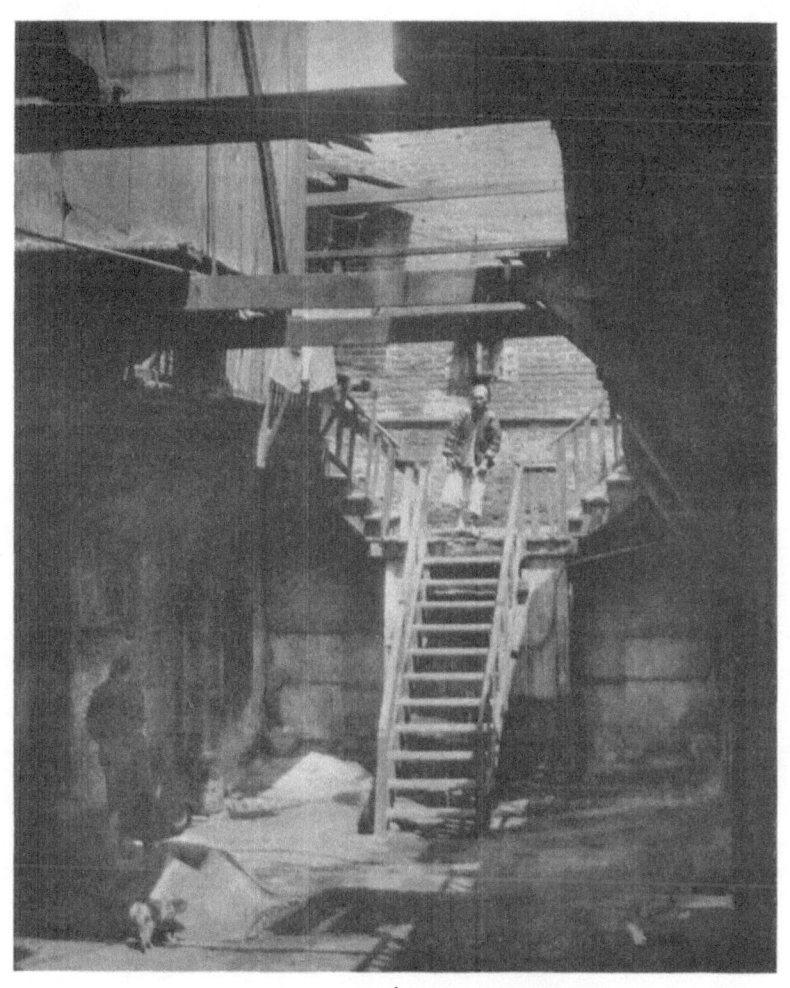

THE DEVIL'S KITCHEN

"THE MOST DILAPIDATED HOLE IN CHINATOWN"

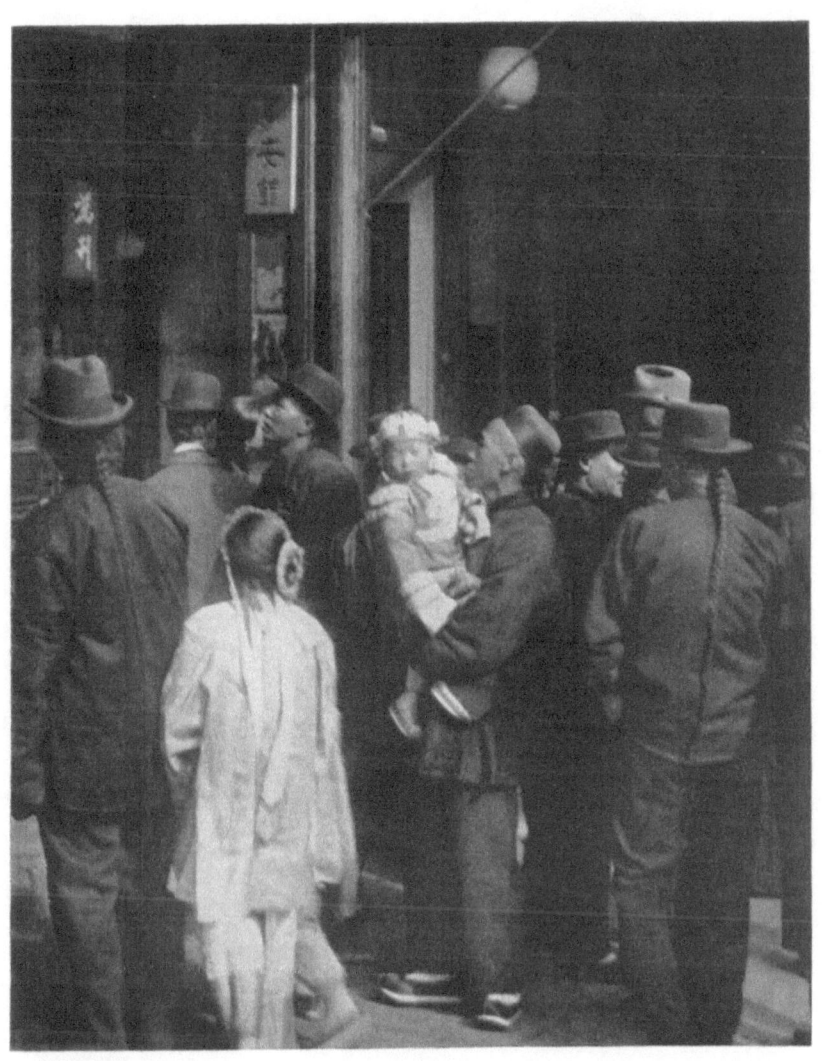

NEW YEAR'S DAY BEFORE THE THEATRE

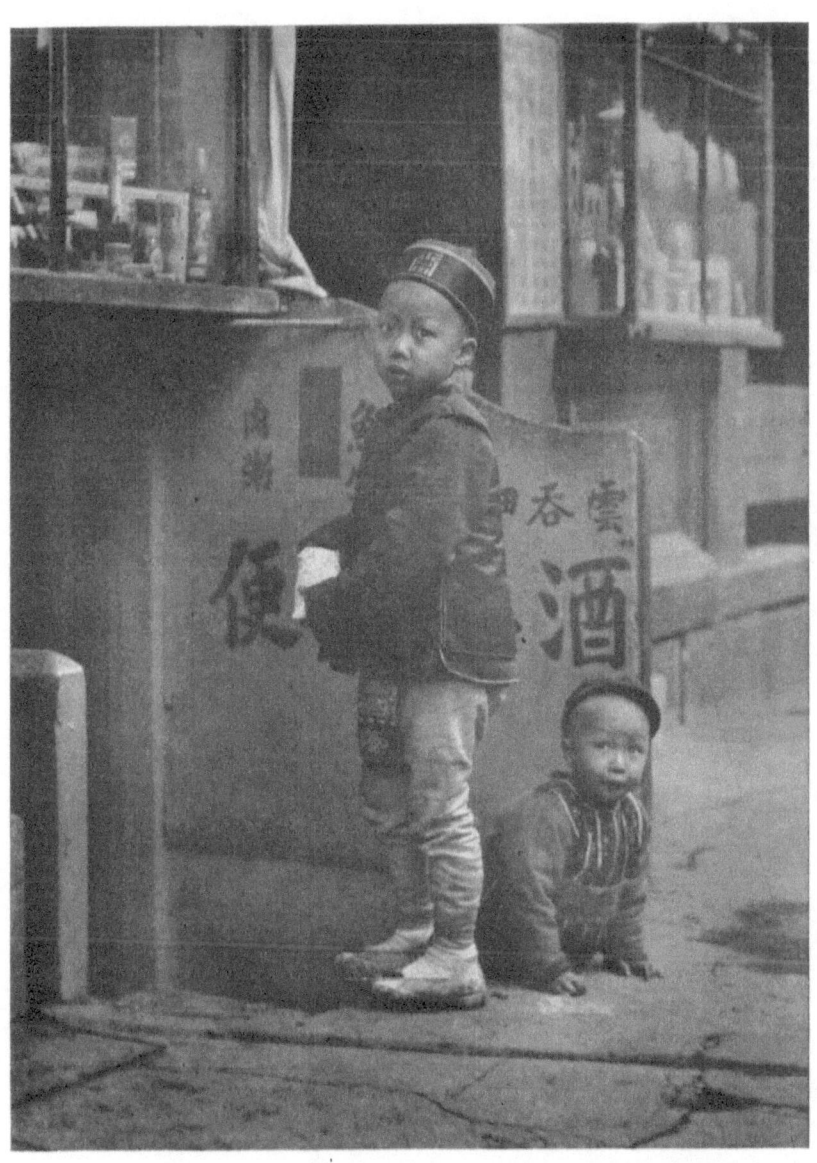

THE CELLAR DOOR

161

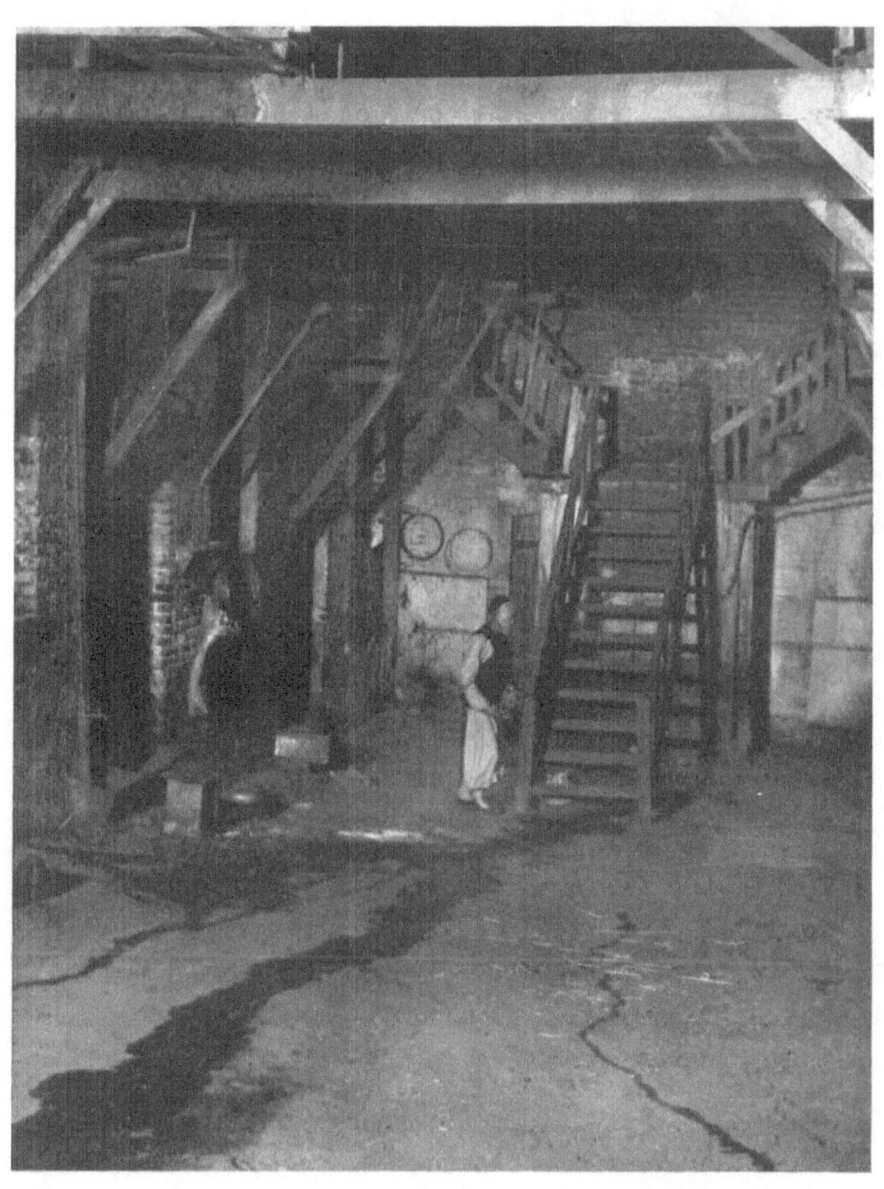

THE DEVIL'S KITCHEN [BY NIGHT]

## CHAPTER NINE

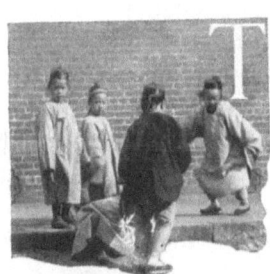

THE world knows from Christian missionaries how little the careless and criminal, among the Chinese at home, value a girl baby. The sale of such children is an established custom — born of the low esteem in which women are held, and of the terrible Chinese famines. Those Californian Chinese, who were degraded enough to stoop to such things, sold these babies into a life of shame. So small was the supply, owing to the difficulty of smuggling women past Federal inspection, that prices were high; it paid a coolie woman to bear female children. A girl four years old, past the delicate stage of infancy, would bring from fifteen hundred to two thousand dollars as a speculation. At thirteen or fourteen, when she was of age to begin making returns to her owner, her price was three thousand. Slavery it was, literal and hopeless; and that in face of the Fourteenth Amendment. The Federal authorities tried to break it up. Pretty generally, they failed. The trouble lay in the Chinese contempt for our courts. Snatch a girl from a brothel, and what happened? A slave from babyhood, kept in ignorance of any other world than that of her brothel, she believed the word of her keeper when he said that white men want girls only to pickle their eyes and eat their brains. First, one must win her from that idea. Then, the master would always bring action in the courts through certain white attorneys unscrupulous enough to take such cases. Chinese witnesses would be found to go upon the stand and swear that this girl was a daughter or niece of the master; and the poor girl, the moment she faced her master in court, would fall into the custom of a lifetime, quail before his eye, and swear falsely that these witnesses told the truth — that she wanted to go back to her "uncle." This system, shameful in our eyes — though indeed there are institutions just as cold-blooded and evil in our own social structure — existed from the first day of Chinatown; exists, I make no doubt, to-day.

From a woman, and she a pretty, fair-spoken Scotch maiden, this slave trade took its hardest blow. Donaldine Cameron was a girl of twenty when she came to take charge of the Presbyterian Mission, which concerns itself especially with the lives and souls of Chinese women. She says herself that she inherited her tastes and talents from a line of Scotch parsons grafted on a line of sheep-stealing Camerons. The spirit in her led her straight to the slave trade. First, as all her predecessors had done, she tried the police and the courts. She found the police inefficient or venal, the courts ineffective. She saw girl after girl, who had welcomed rescue in the beginning, crumple up on the witness stand and swear herself back into slavery.

Nevertheless, Miss Cameron kept on, raiding and fighting in the courts. In a warfare of ten years, she won a kind of Fabian victory. She usually lost her girl in the end, but before that end she had cost the owner dear in smashed doors, valuable property kept idle, disturbance of business, and the heavy fees which the white attorneys used to exact from the Chinese. Playing her desperate lone hand, she reduced the traffic by about one-half.

Our lives in old San Francisco were all tinged a little with romance; but I can think of no life among us which so quivered with adventure as hers. Would that I could convey the quaint, workaday style in which this Scotch gentlewoman related her adventures — the material of a dime novel, the manner of a housewife telling about her marketing. During one raid, she met at the door of the brothel some unforeseen barrier which delayed the attack. As she waited for the axman, she looked through the latticed window upon a confusion of painted Chinese women, all squalling together. From this group, a girl disentangled herself and came running, her arms outstretched, toward the raiders. It was the girl they had come to rescue; and by this fatal slip, born of over-eagerness, she revealed that she was first cause of the raid. The slave master perceived it, too; before Miss Cameron's eyes he knocked her down and dragged her by the hair through a sliding panel, which opened at his touch. When at last Miss Cameron gained entrance, she found a dozen passages leading confusingly from this secret door; the inmates had lost themselves in the Third Circle. She never saw that girl again; but months later the underground gossip of Chinatown brought Miss Cameron the end of the tale. The master had beaten her to death in the presence of his other women.

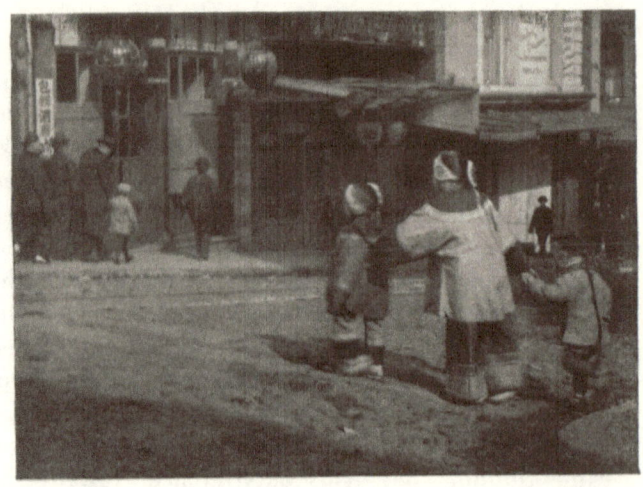

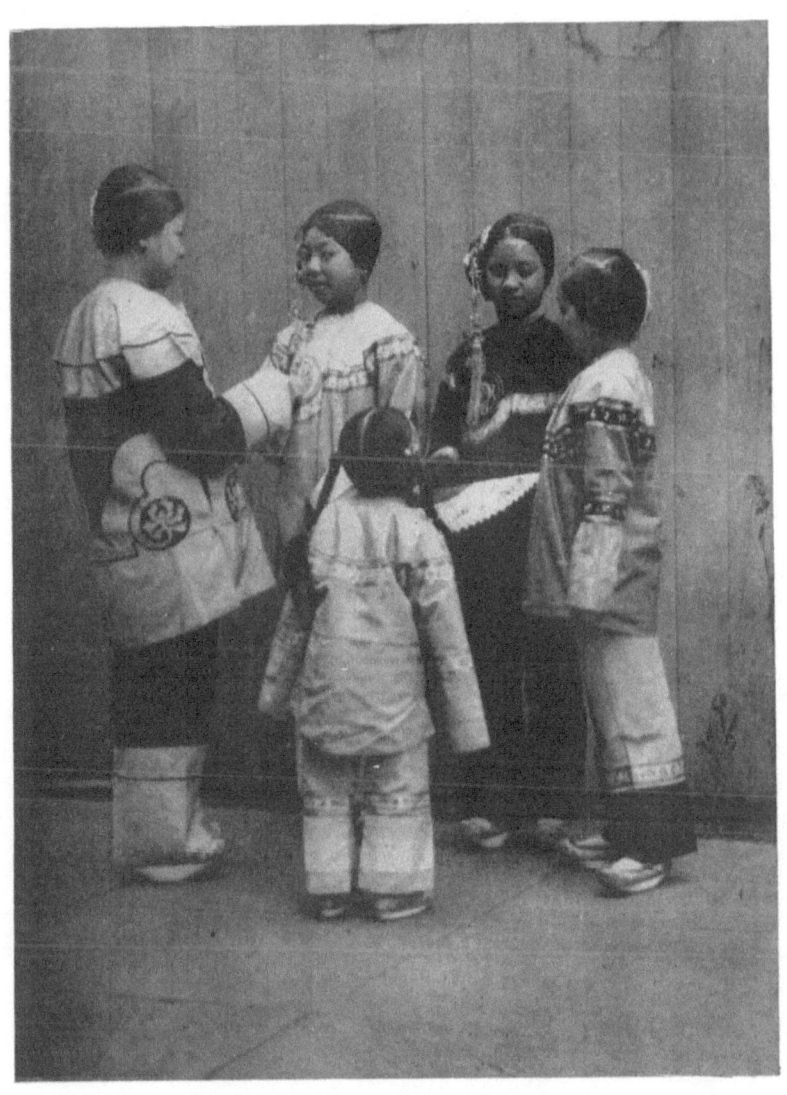

RESCUED SLAVE GIRLS

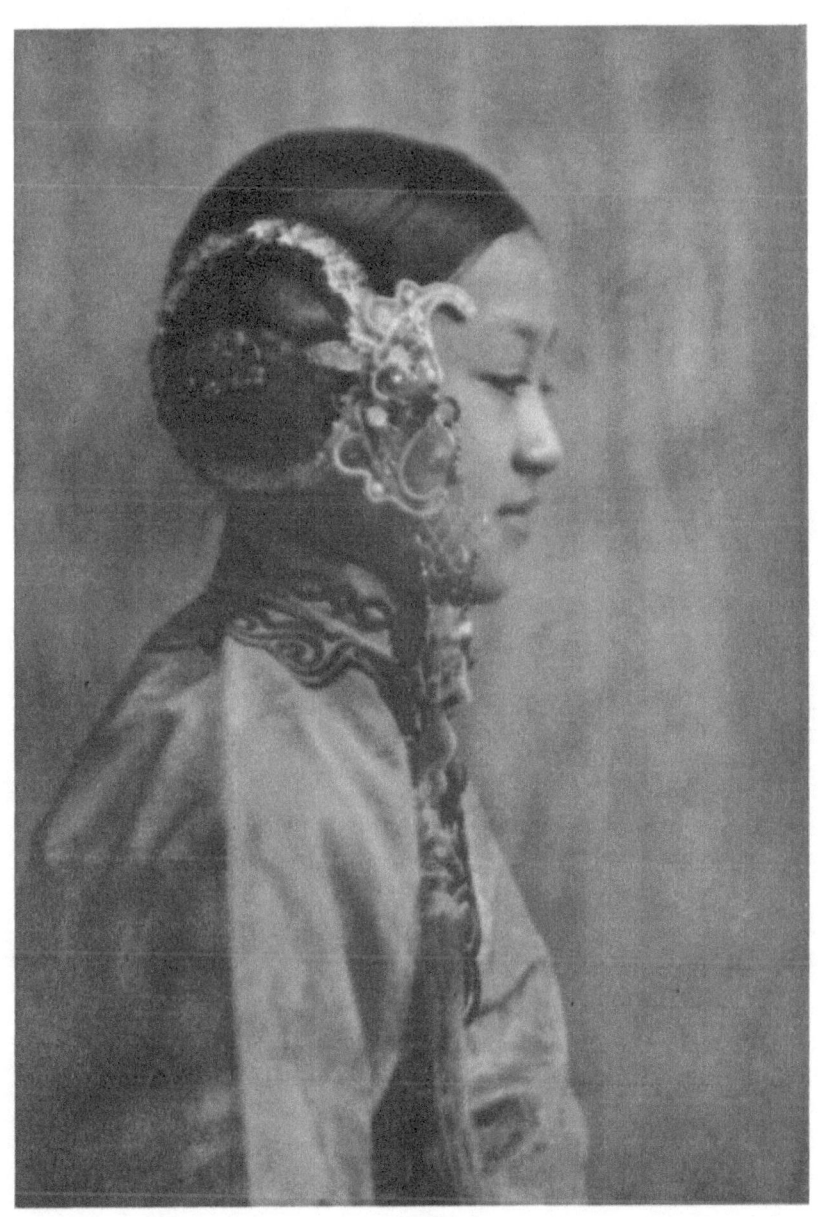

LITTLE TEA ROSE
**173**

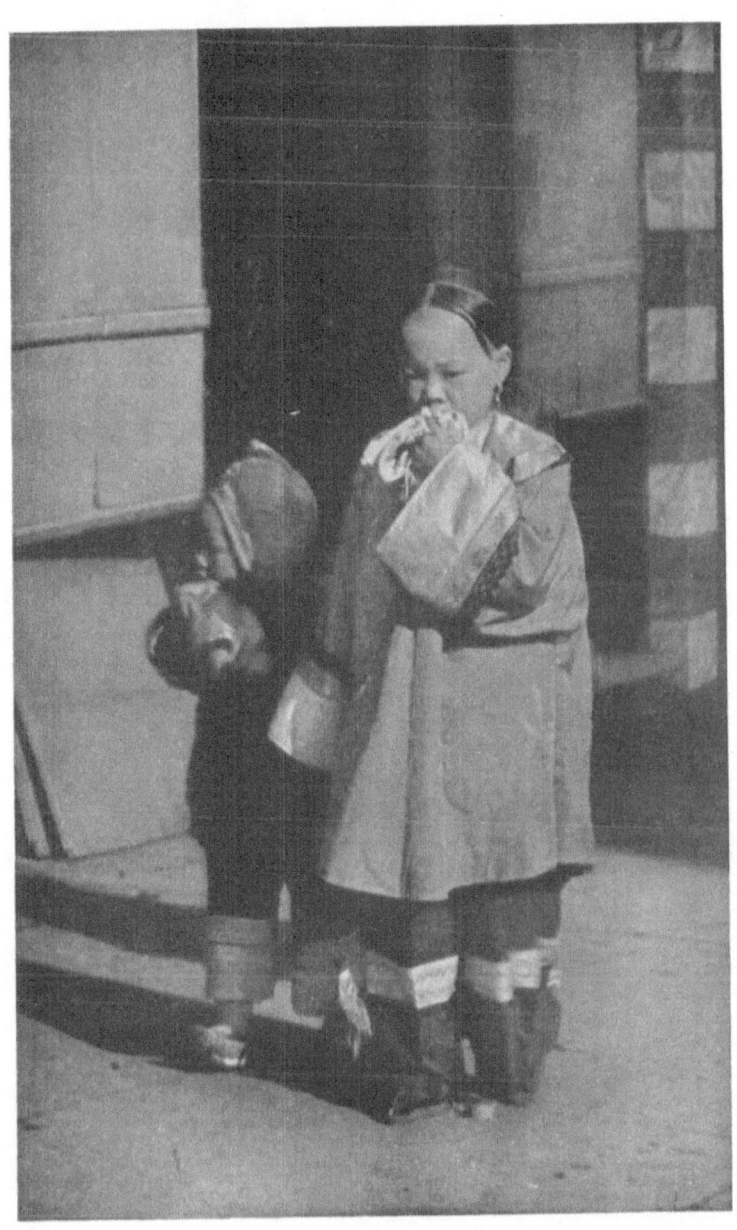

RETURNING HOME

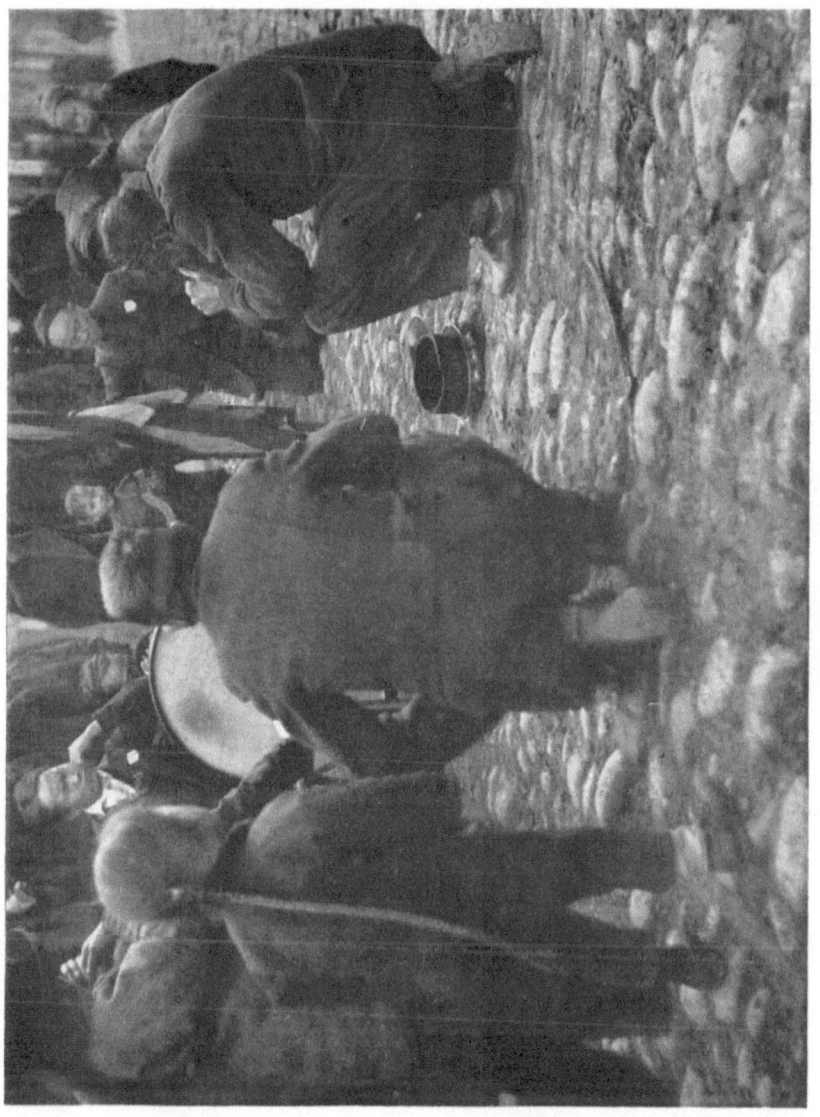

THE CHINESE SALVATION ARMY

EVERY NIGHT THIS HANDFUL OF CONVERTS SANG
AND EXHORTED IN CHINESE AND ENGLISH

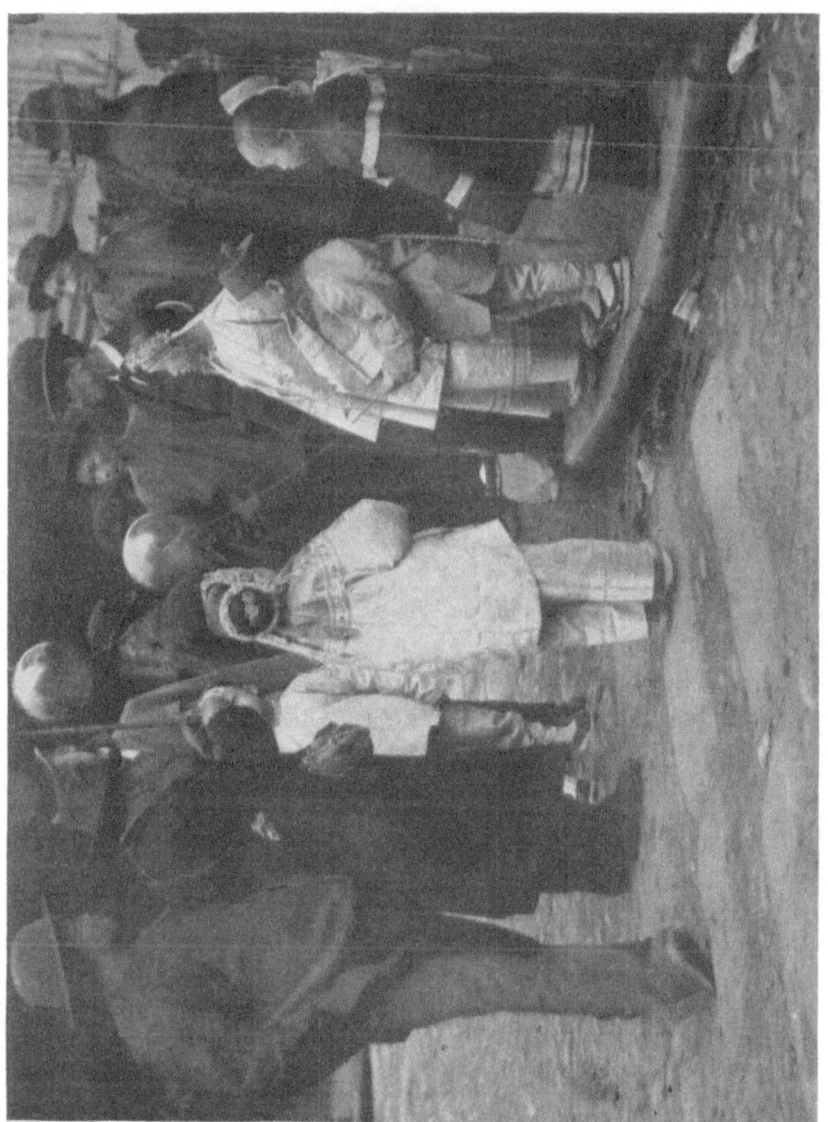

179

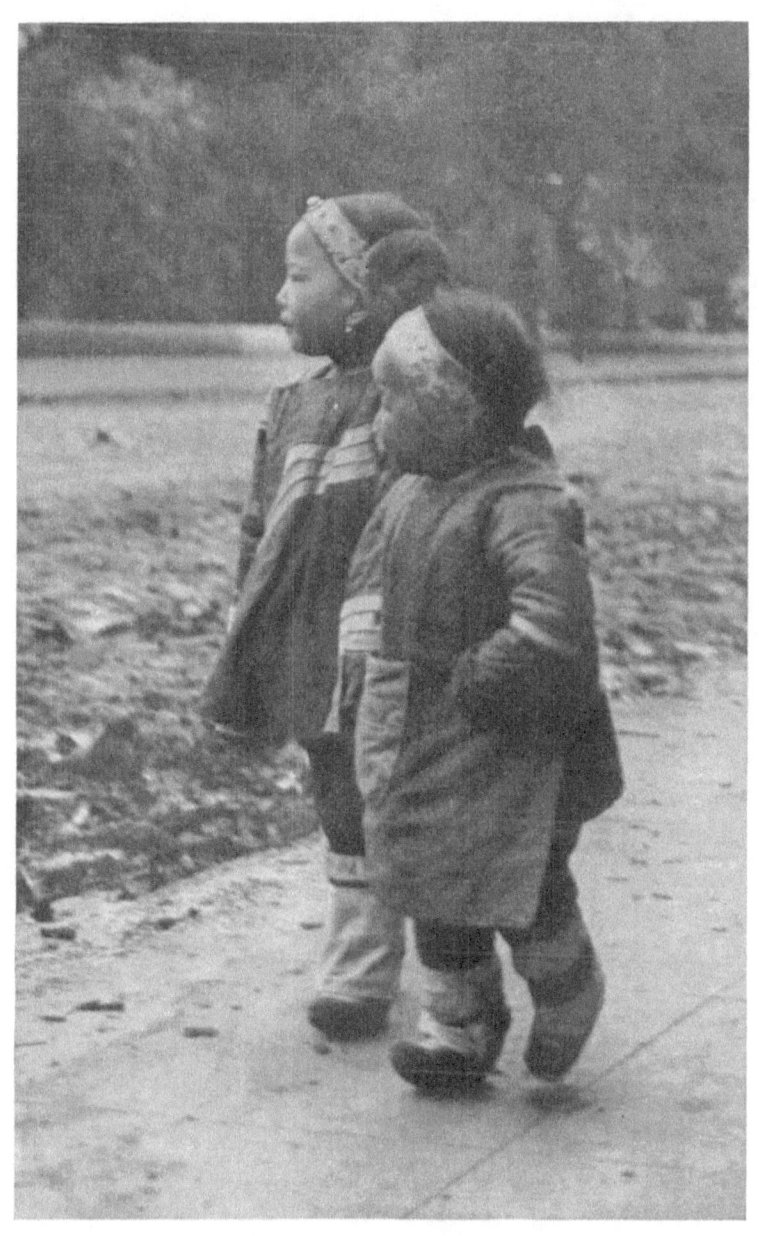

A STROLL ON THE PLAZA

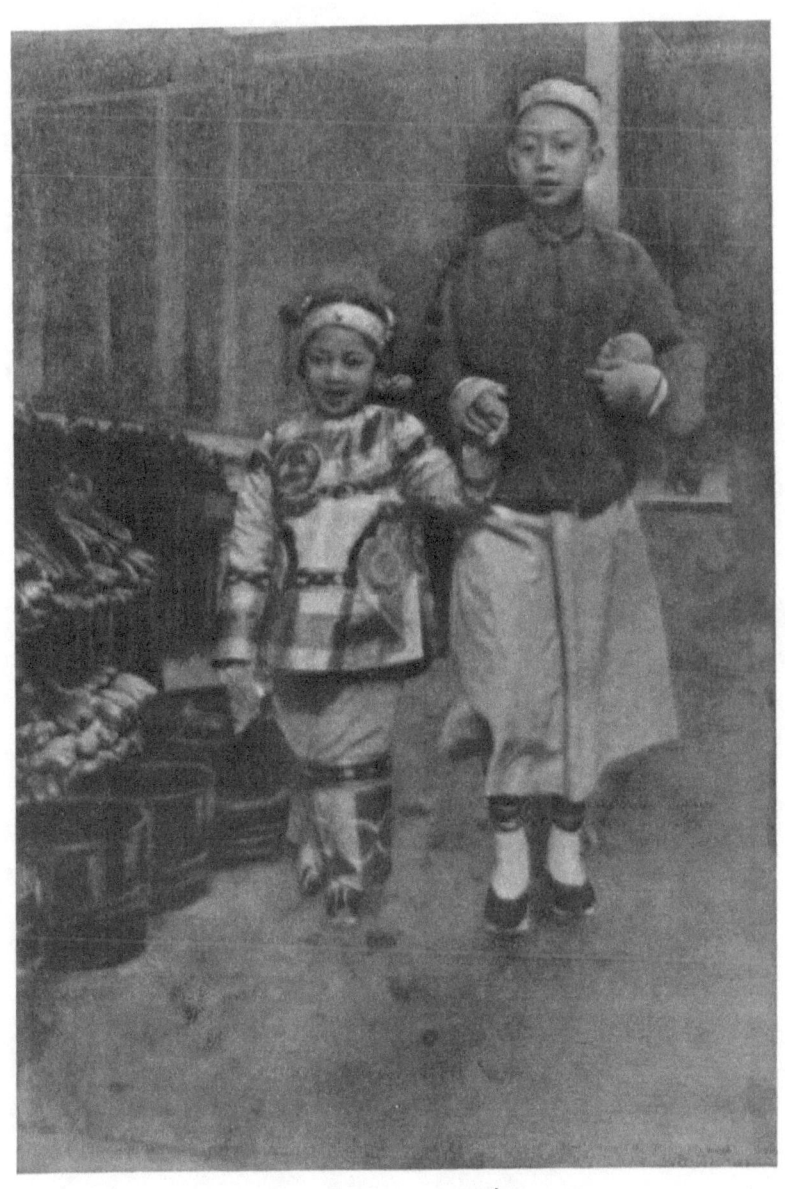

BUYING NEW YEAR'S GIFTS

## CHAPTER TEN

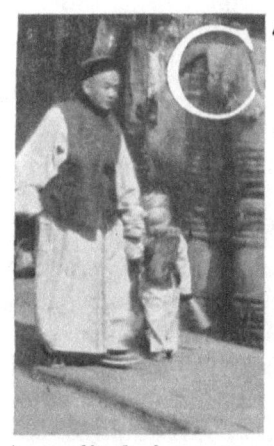

CAN the lover of Old China-town ever fail to keep in memory its characters and . scenes, the gay colors and mysterious shadows? Unforgettable is the figure of the strangest of the white inhabitants of Chinatown who was known as the Emperor of the Universe. He was the mildest, gentlest paranoiac that ever followed the moon. For years he walked the streets; a tall old man, with one of the sparse beards which Heaven grants to but few Chinese. Always, as he walked, he smoked a long, curved pipe and turned a look of kindly disdain upon the populace. He believed that all these Whites and Chinese were his subjects; but he was a benevolent ruler, well content with his domain. For that reason, and also because everyone liked him, no one ever took the trouble to lock him up. The Central Police Station came to inhabit the Hall of Justice across Portsmouth Square. At four o'clock on fine days, the downtown squad used to deploy on the sidewalk. The Emperor was always there. He would walk down the line with the air of a general reviewing his troops, salute formally and march back to Chinatown. When the captain in command was good-natured, he let his policemen return the salute — which they did with all gravity in the world.

Who can ever forget the pipe-bowl mender, *the* pipe-bowl mender who sat in the same spot — on Dupont Street a few doors from Jackson — for a decade long? A picture always, what with his bowstring bits, his tiny hammers, his leather cases, he was most a picture on cold days when he got out his marten-lined jacket from the family inheritance, and his fur cap. In the short-lived drama, "The First Born," which so enchanted San Francisco, Power the author and Benrimo the actor made this pipe-bowl mender chorus to all the things which happened on a certain tragic Chinatown night. Who forgets the Pekin Two Knife Man who used to perform a sword dance of the Old Empire? Who forgets that withered wisp of a Confucian priest whose task it was to gather day by day all the papers on the streets, that the name of the god-sage might never be profaned? Who forgets Ah Chic of the splendid, noble face, the greatest actor (I verily believe) of all his time in America — Ah Chic who lived and died in the Jackson Street theatre, playing seven nights a week for the pure love of playing, to coolies who could never understand? Who forgets the lantern maker, he who plaited moons of red and gold delight out of paper and

# ARNOLD GENTHE

bamboo strips, betraying the artist in all those devices by which he made each one a little different from the other?

Gentle figures whose memory will linger all the more unforgettably, since their old environment is gone.

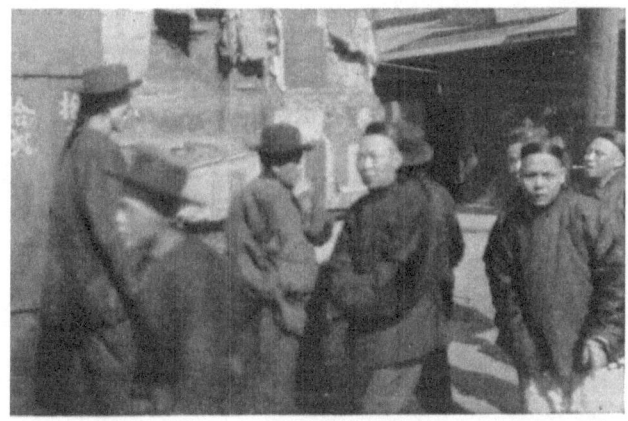

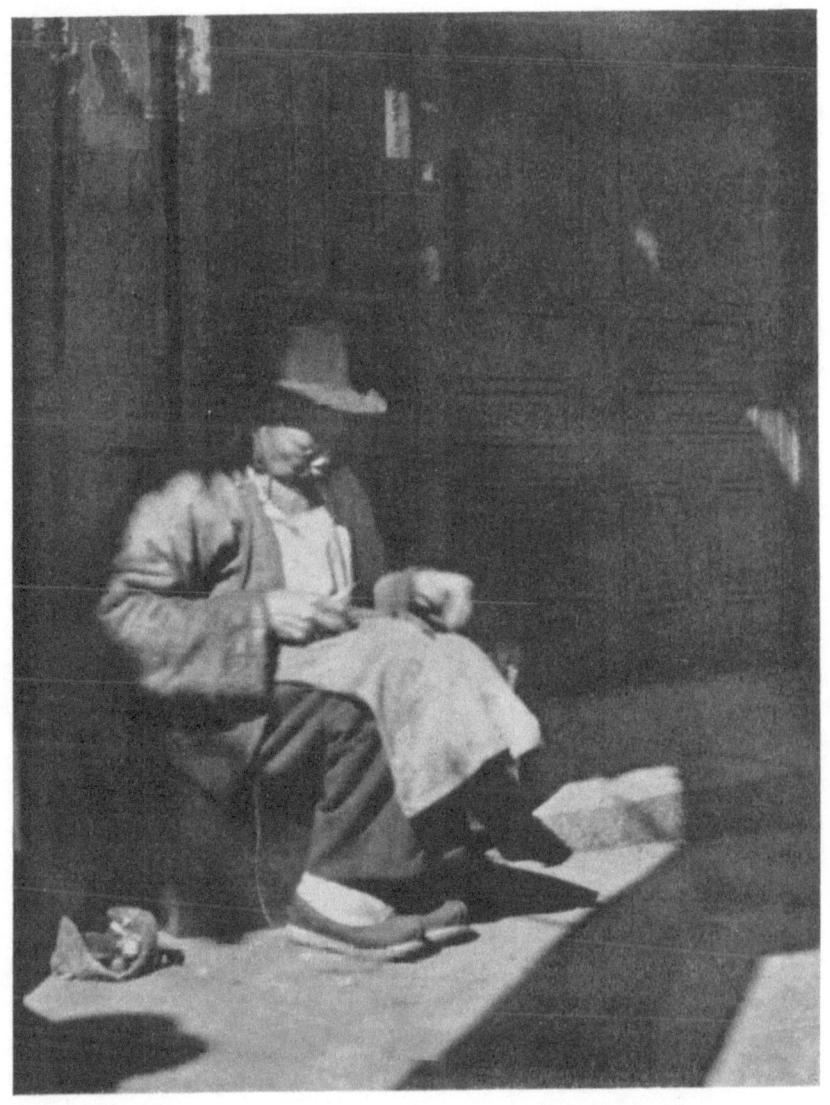

THE PIPE-BOWL MENDER

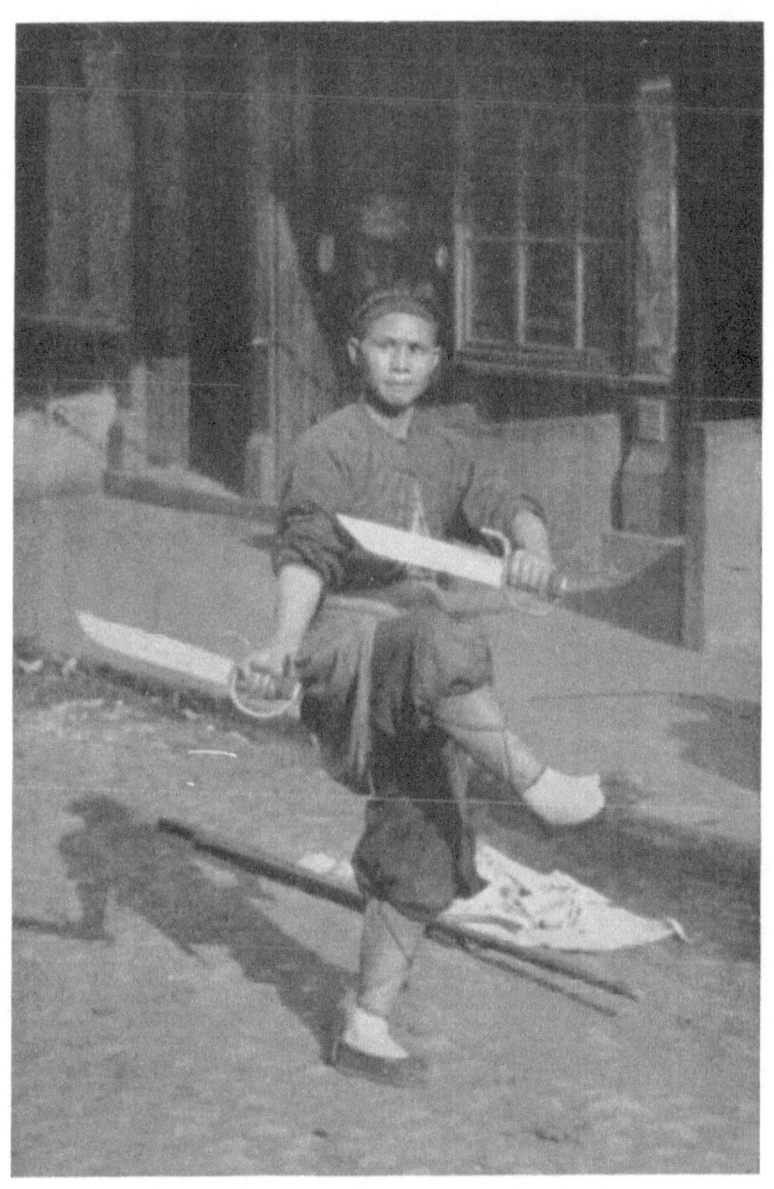

THE SWORD DANCER

"YOU GIVE ME TWO BITS, I MAKE HIM FINE"

191

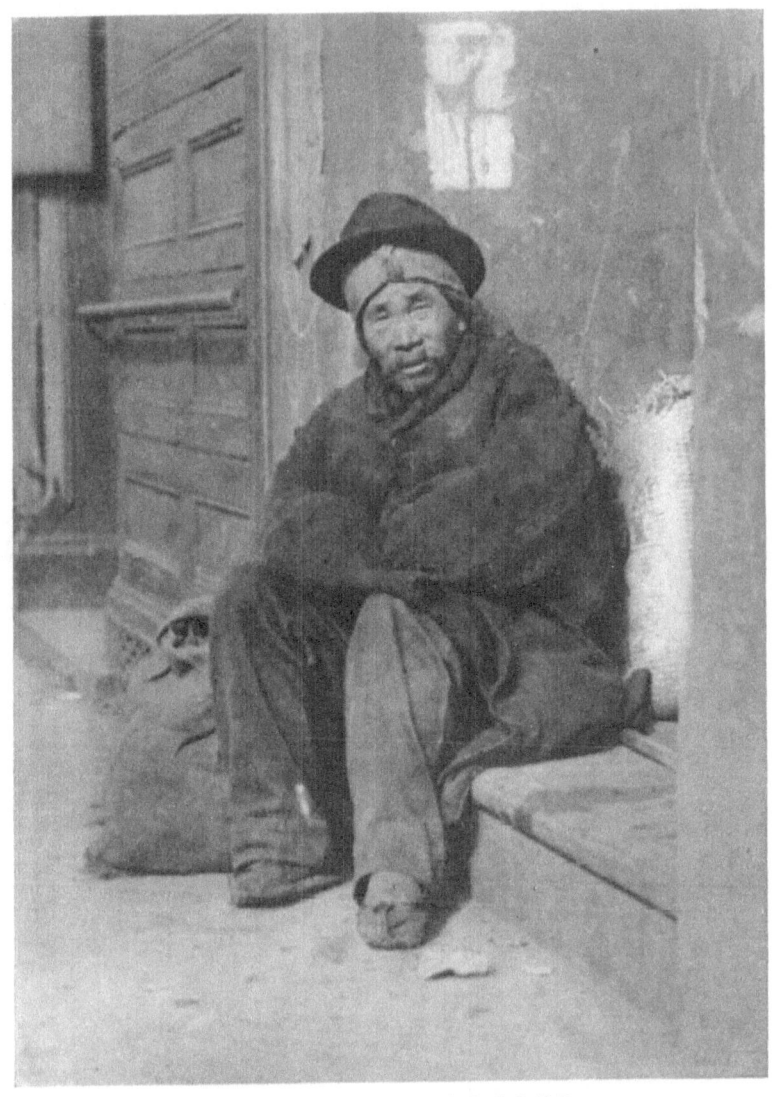

THE PAPER GATHERER

193

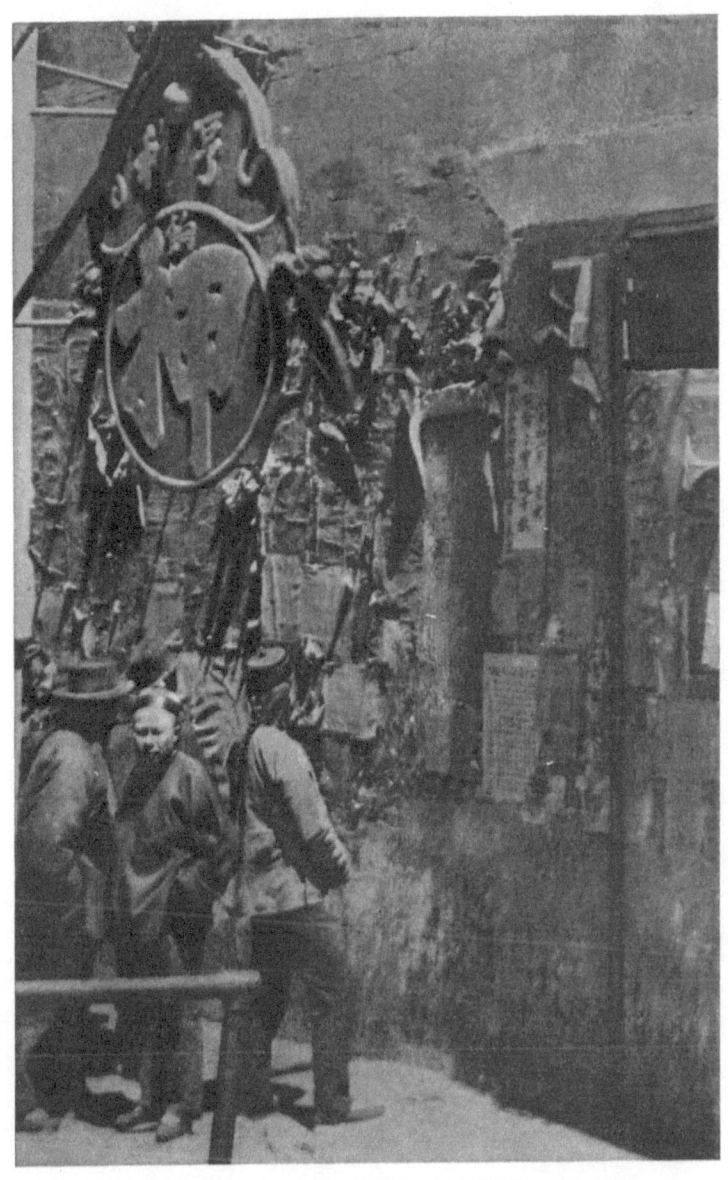

THE SIGN OF THE PAWN SHOP

195

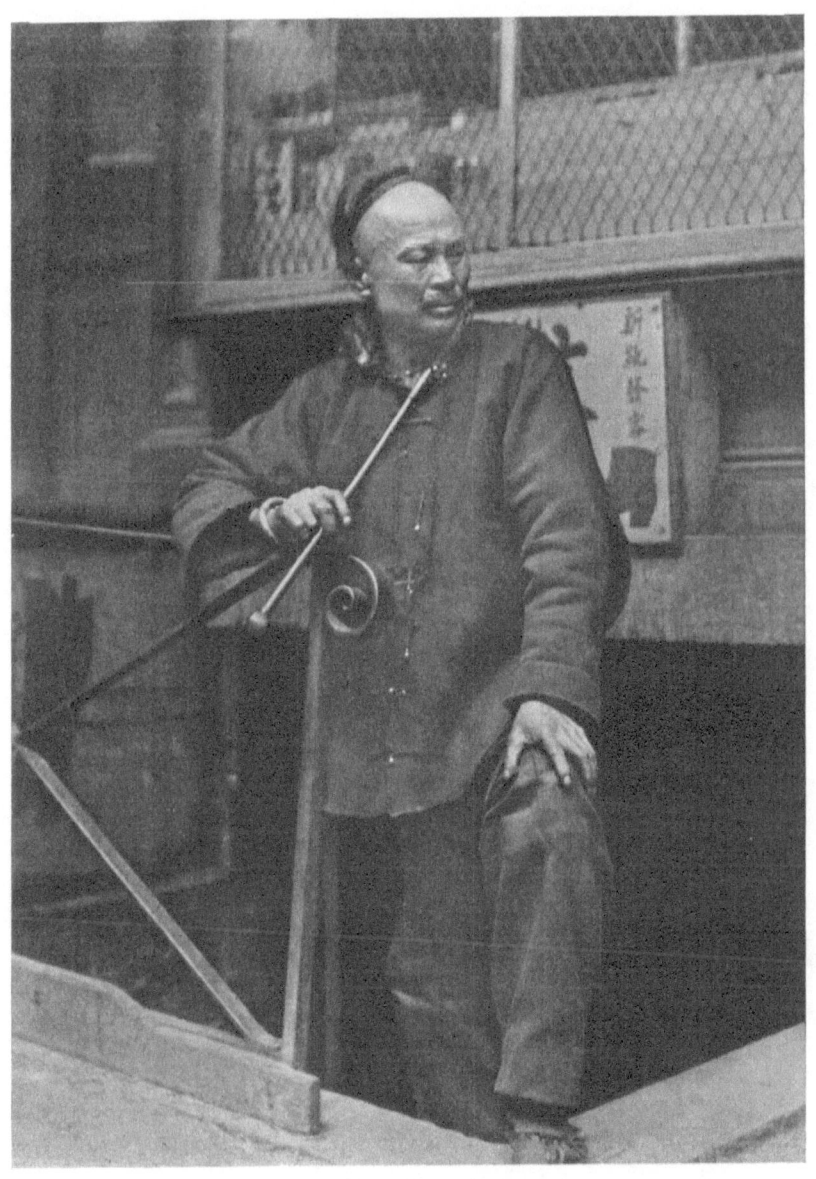

THE SHOE MAKER

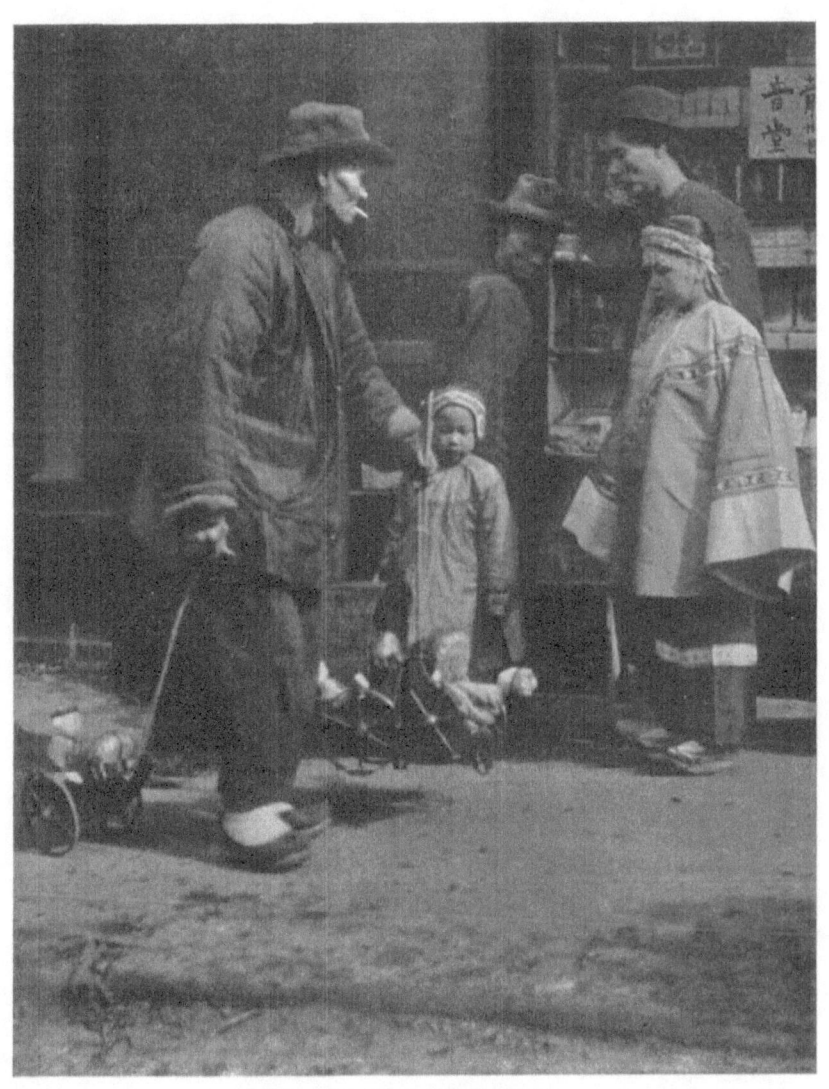

THE TOY PEDDLER

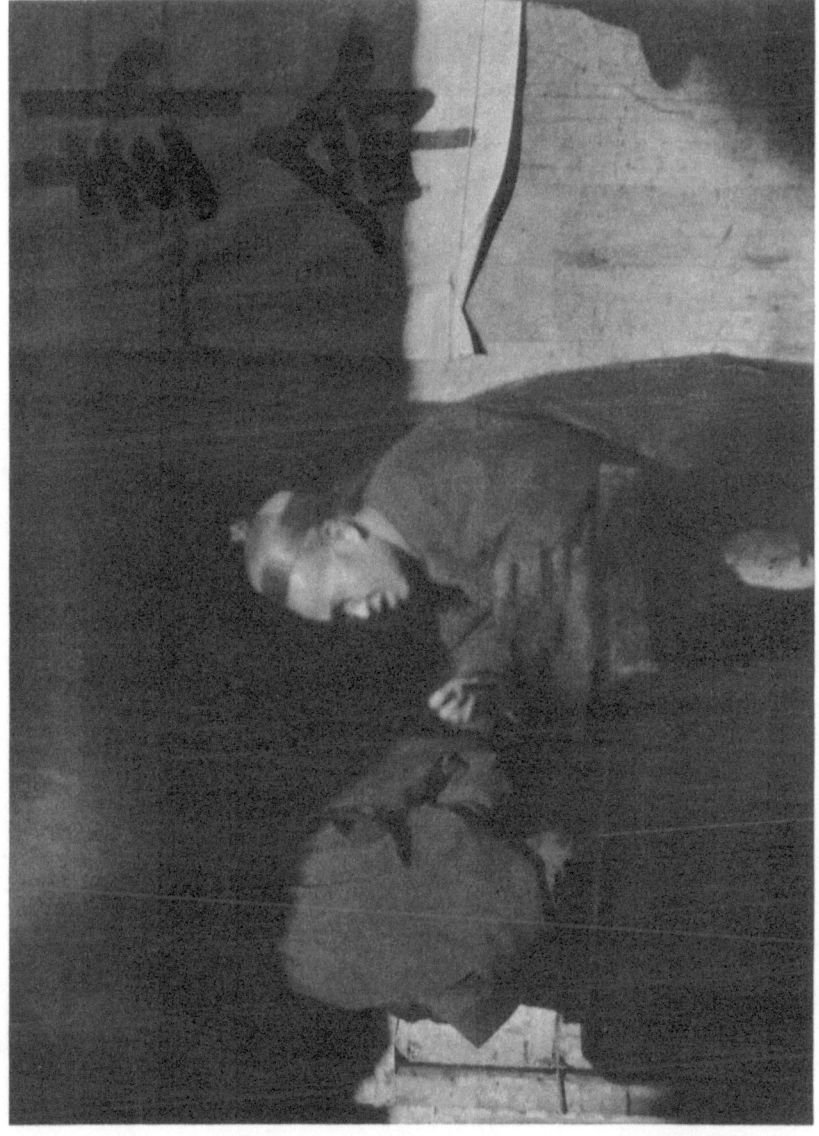

THE FORTUNE TELLER

"BY-AND-BY, YOU CATCHEE PLENTY MONEY, MAYBE"

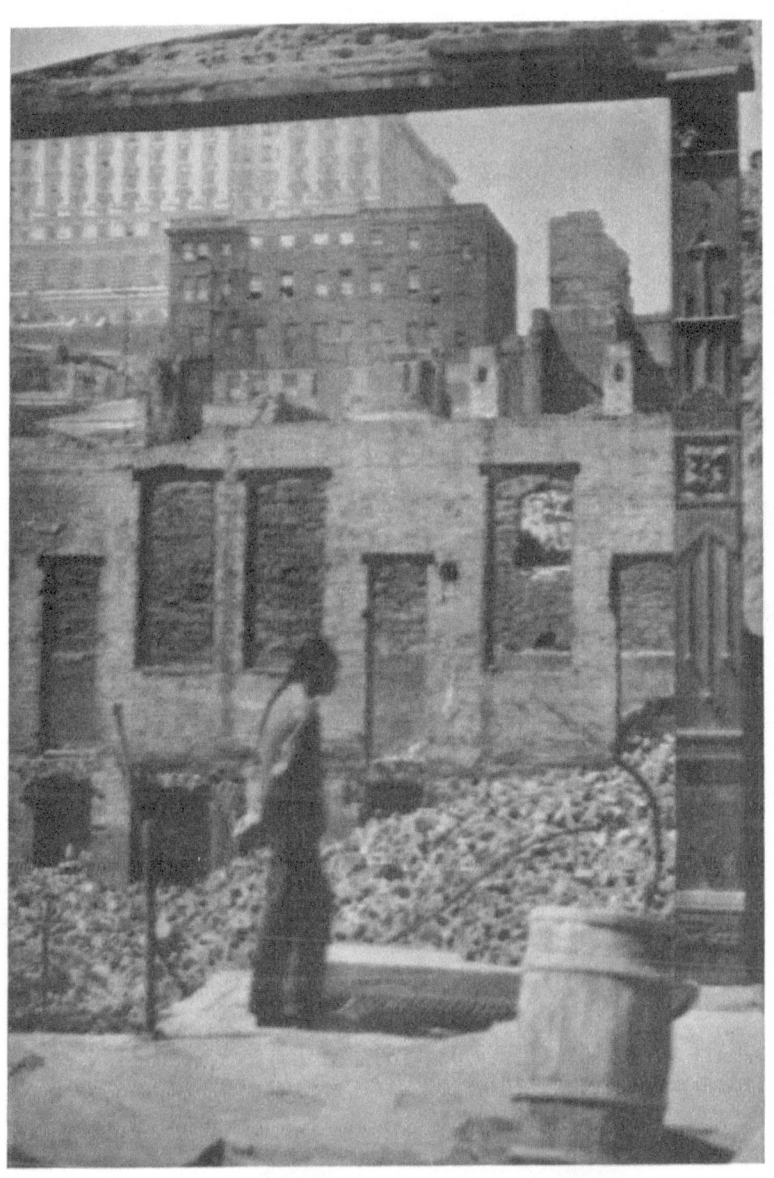

AFTER THE FIRE, 1906

[THE FAIRMONT HOTEL IN THE DISTANCE]

# POSTSCRIPT

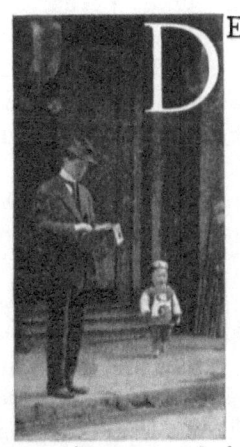

**D**EAR WILL IRWIN: It was the evening before my departure from San Francisco, just about a year ago. I had strolled down to Chinatown for a last visit. In the glare of blazing shop fronts, in the noise of chugging automobiles carrying sightseers, I again, as so many times before, found myself trying to see the old mellowness of dimly-lit alleys, the mystery of shadowy figures shuffling along silently. I was interrupted by the officious voice of a guide: "Show you all the sights of Chineetown, Sir! Opium-dens, slave-girls, jewelry-shops, joss-houses, everything." The idea of seeing Chinatown for once as an average tourist appealed to me. I followed the guide.

At last I, who for years had tried to deceive myself with sentimental persistency — just as one searches for traces of lost beauty in a beloved face — was forced to admit that Old Chinatown, the city we loved so well, is no more. A new City, cleaner, better, brighter, has risen in its place.

[ *205* ]

# OLD CHINATOWN

On brilliantly illuminated streets, smoothly as-
phalted, filled with crowds in American clothes,
stand imposing bazaars of an architecture that
never was, blazing in myriads of electric lights.
Costly silk embroideries in gaudy colors, porcelains
of florid design, bronzes with hand-made patina,
and a host of gay Chinese and Japanese wares which
the wise Oriental manufactures for us barbarians,
tempt the tourist to enter, while inside cash-registers
and department-store manners, replacing abacus
and old-time courtesy, indicate up-to-date methods.
In one store the Chinese owner even wears a proud
tuxedo. Yet even to-day, in these ware-houses of
quite modern Oriental art, as well as in the modest
store of the small dealer next door, may the patient
searcher discover a precious bit of lacquer, a
charming piece of brocade.

The theatre, in which Ah Chic had delighted our
hearts with his wonderful art, and where so many
times we had tried to discover expressive rhythm and
leit-motifs in the din of the Chinese orchestra, has
ceased to exist. The endowment is lacking. An
"Oriental Theater," a moving picture show, fills its
place. Nothing is Chinese there except part of the
audience. The joss houses where young and old
used to worship strange divinities, are rebuilt with
some lavishness, and the old gods, attired in bright
new robes and glittering tinsel, are once more
ensconced in their gilded temples. But who may
guess their sacred trepidation? Had they not lost a
great deal of their erstwhile prestige, when ignomin-
iously they failed to save themselves and Chinatown
in the great fire! The Street of the Gamblers has

become a street of indifferent rooming-houses, and the Street of the Slave Girls has been translated into unsavory French. Opium dens are invisible, since the police has closed them all and destroyed in a virtuous holocaust — just as was done throughout all China — every pipe they could gather. Thanks to the Police and Board of Health, all that remains of the underground passages, where crime and mystery lurked in impenetrable shadows, is the lurid tale of the guide. In the goldsmith-shops on Dupont and Jackson Streets the hammers are busy, for Chinese vanity continues to demand gold ornaments decorated with jade. Yet old patterns and careful workmanship are often giving way to new designs and indifferent methods. The most noteworthy sight of the new Chinatown seems to be the small store where souvenirs of the great fire are sold by an American woman whose sister bears an illustrious name and whose husband is a Chinaman.

Of the old life of Chinatown only three things remain unchanged: in the drug-stores, just as of old, aromatic herbs and unknown roots, gall of bear and horn of deer, small dried animals of land and sea and other weird things can be purchased, to be concocted into an all-curing tea; the pawn-shop sign still indicates the place where old embroideries, fur-lined coats and jade bracelets have found a temporary abiding place; and the inevitable Tong feuds carried on by lawless highbinders still furnish excitement to the Quarter and thrilling reading for the papers. It was in one of these recent Tong wars that our philosophical friend the old Fortune-Teller was killed by a hired assassin.

# OLD CHINATOWN

Do you remember how his prediction "by-an'-by you catchee plenty money, may-be" used to appeal to you? As for the restaurants, there are several where Chinese tea and sweetmeats and Chop Suey are served to tourists; the old Far Low restaurant has even made quite a laudable attempt to re-establish the old order. Alas! it is in vain. The charm, the color, the atmosphere are gone. And that is true of the whole Quarter.

We both were bad prophets when on that memorable night five years ago, under the ruined walls of St. Mary's, we discussed the future of the newly rising Chinatown. We did not foresee that a force more destructive than fire, the spirit of revolution that has made the Chinese Republic a reality, was to abolish in a short time, what we had hoped would remain Chinese. Now everywhere American clothes replace the silken gowns of old, and a general ambition to be "American" in manners as well as in appearance is evident.

When the Chinese, from consul down to coolie, as outward sign of having broken with the traditions of their country, cut off their queues, Old Chinatown died. And if we, you with your pen and I with my camera, have caught some of its old picturesque charm, adding perhaps here and there a touch of poetry to the mere fact, we may in all modesty feel that we have done something of value, for which San Francisco's friends will be grateful.

ARNOLD GENTHE.

1912.

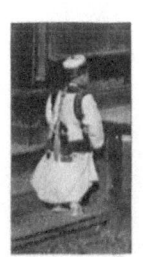

www.ingramcontent.com/pod-product-compliance
Lightning Source LLC
Chambersburg PA
CBHW020902180526
45163CB00007B/2596